Knowledge Graph Basics

Understanding, Designing, and Implementing Graph-Based Systems

James Acklin

Copyright Page

Table of Contents

Preface

In today's world, data is ubiquitous, complex, and interconnected. As businesses, researchers, and technologists grapple with the ever-growing volume and variety of information, there is a pressing need for systems that can meaningfully represent and analyze this complexity. Knowledge graphs have emerged as a powerful solution, enabling us to organize, connect, and derive insights from data in ways that traditional methods cannot achieve. This book, **"Knowledge Graph Basics: Understanding, Designing, and Implementing Graph-Based Systems,"** is a comprehensive guide for anyone looking to understand and leverage the potential of knowledge graphs.

The idea for this book was born out of a growing demand for accessible, practical resources on knowledge graphs. While the topic has been extensively researched and discussed in academic and technical circles, many newcomers find the subject daunting. Our goal is to demystify knowledge graphs and present their principles, design processes, and applications in a clear and approachable manner. Whether you are a data scientist, software engineer, business analyst, or simply curious about the field, this book provides a roadmap to understanding and building graph-based systems.

The book is structured to guide readers through the entire lifecycle of a knowledge graph project, from foundational concepts to advanced implementations. It begins by introducing the basics: what knowledge graphs are, how they have evolved, and why they are increasingly relevant in today's data-driven world. Readers will then explore the core components of knowledge graphs, including graph theory, ontologies, and semantic representations. With this foundation in place, we delve into the practical aspects of designing, building, and implementing knowledge graphs, covering key topics like data integration, graph modeling, and querying.

One of the unique strengths of knowledge graphs lies in their versatility, and we have dedicated a section of the book to exploring their applications across various domains. From powering search engines and recommendation systems to enabling breakthroughs in healthcare and finance, knowledge graphs are transforming industries. In addition, we address the challenges and limitations associated with their design and maintenance, offering insights into scalability, performance optimization, and ethical considerations.

This book also includes a hands-on guide, providing practical examples and step-by-step instructions for building your own knowledge graph. By combining theoretical knowledge with real-world applications, we hope to empower readers to apply these concepts to their own projects and innovate in their respective fields.

Writing this book has been a rewarding journey, and it is our hope that it serves as a valuable resource for anyone interested in this transformative technology. We have aimed to strike a balance between clarity and depth, ensuring that readers of varying backgrounds and expertise levels can benefit from its content.

Finally, we would like to express our gratitude to the countless researchers, developers, and thought leaders who have contributed to the advancement of knowledge graphs. Their work has laid the foundation for the ideas and practices shared in this book. We also thank our readers for embarking on this journey with us, and we look forward to seeing the incredible solutions and systems you will create with the knowledge gained from this book.

Welcome to the world of knowledge graphs—an exciting intersection of data, technology, and innovation. Let's begin!

Chapter 1: Introduction to Knowledge Graphs

Welcome to knowledge graphs! In this chapter, we'll explore the basics of what knowledge graphs are, how they came to be, and why they are increasingly important in today's data-driven world. We'll keep things conversational and approachable, so you can grasp these foundational concepts without feeling overwhelmed. Let's dive in!

1.1 What is a Knowledge Graph?

A knowledge graph is a way to organize and connect information that reflects the relationships between entities in a structured, meaningful way. It isn't just about storing data like a spreadsheet or a database table. Instead, it's about connecting the dots, showing how entities relate to one another, and enabling systems to understand and process those connections just as humans do. Let's break it down step by step and explore the essential aspects of what a knowledge graph is and how it works.

A knowledge graph consists of **nodes** (representing entities like people, places, or objects) and **edges** (representing relationships or interactions between these entities). But what makes a knowledge graph special isn't just this structure. It's also the **semantics** that are embedded into the graph. Semantics give context and meaning to the relationships, helping systems and users interpret the data accurately.

For instance, if you see "Paris is the capital of France" in a knowledge graph:

- "Paris" is a node (an entity).

- "France" is another node (another entity).

- "Is the capital of" is the edge (the relationship between them).

What makes this powerful is that the graph understands what these entities are and how they connect. "Paris" isn't just a string of text; it's recognized as a city. "France" is identified as a country. The edge "is the capital of" carries specific meaning, enabling both machines and humans to infer knowledge from the graph.

What Sets Knowledge Graphs Apart from Databases?

To understand knowledge graphs better, let's contrast them with traditional databases. Databases are excellent for storing and retrieving structured data in tabular formats, but they struggle when the relationships between data points become complex or when the data changes dynamically.

Knowledge graphs solve these challenges by:

1. Representing information as a network rather than isolated tables.

2. Focusing on the connections between data points.

3. Allowing for evolution without major restructuring. New entities and relationships can be added seamlessly.

For example, in a relational database, you might have a "Countries" table and a "Capitals" table, and you'd need to write queries to join them and extract relationships. In a knowledge graph, these relationships are naturally part of the structure, making it much more intuitive to query and explore.

A Practical Example

Let's consider a social network like LinkedIn. In a traditional database, you'd store users, their connections, and their professional details in separate tables. But what if you wanted to answer a query like: "Show me all the people in my network who work in tech and live in New York City"?

In a relational database, this would involve complex joins and conditions, and as the data grows, it becomes slow and cumbersome. With a knowledge graph, this query becomes straightforward because:

- Users are **nodes**.

- Attributes like "industry" or "location" are part of the graph's structure.

- Connections between users (edges) carry meaning, such as "works at" or "lives in."

Here's an example of how this might look in a knowledge graph query:

```
# A SPARQL query to find people in your network who
work in tech and live in New York
PREFIX foaf: <http://xmlns.com/foaf/0.1/>
PREFIX schema: <http://schema.org/>

SELECT ?person
WHERE {
  ?person schema:worksFor ?company .
  ?person schema:livesIn "New York City" .
  ?company schema:industry "Tech" .
}
```

This query leverages the relationships in the graph to find exactly what you need, without complicated joins or filtering logic.

How Do Knowledge Graphs Work?

At a high level, knowledge graphs operate by organizing data into a graph structure and enriching it with semantic meaning. The steps involved include:

1. Defining the Schema: A schema defines the structure of the graph—what entities and relationships exist and how they relate to one another. This can be formalized using standards like RDF (Resource Description Framework) or OWL (Web Ontology Language).

2. Populating the Graph: Data is ingested from various sources, including structured databases, unstructured text, APIs, and more. This data is converted into nodes and edges according to the schema.

3. Querying the Graph: Users or applications query the graph using languages like SPARQL, which is specifically designed for graph databases. The queries can be as simple as retrieving a single entity or as complex as inferring new knowledge based on existing relationships.

4. Reasoning and Inference: Advanced knowledge graphs use logic and rules to infer new facts from existing data. For example, if the graph knows that "John works for Company X"

and "Company X is in San Francisco," it can infer that "John is likely in San Francisco."

Real-World Use Case: Google Knowledge Graph

When you search for something on Google, like "Leonardo da Vinci," you'll often see a box on the side with information about him—his works, birthplace, important dates, and related people. This is powered by Google's Knowledge Graph.

Here's how it works behind the scenes:

- Entities: Leonardo da Vinci, Mona Lisa, Renaissance.

- Relationships: "Leonardo da Vinci painted Mona Lisa."

- Semantics: Google's graph understands that "painted" signifies a relationship between an artist and artwork.

This structured information enhances search results, enabling Google to provide direct answers rather than just links to web pages.

Exercise: Building a Simple Knowledge Graph

Let's construct a basic knowledge graph using Python and a library like rdflib. Suppose we want to model a graph about people, their cities, and professions.

```python
from rdflib import Graph, Literal, RDF, URIRef,
Namespace

# Create a new graph
g = Graph()

# Define a namespace
EX = Namespace("http://example.org/")

# Add entities (nodes)
john = URIRef(EX.John)
new_york = URIRef(EX.NewYork)
engineer = URIRef(EX.Engineer)

# Add relationships (edges)
g.add((john, RDF.type, EX.Person))
g.add((john, EX.livesIn, new_york))
```

```
g.add((john, EX.profession, engineer))

# Serialize the graph to see its structure
print(g.serialize(format="turtle").decode("utf-8"))
```

This code snippet defines a simple graph where John is a person, lives in New York, and works as an engineer. The graph can now be expanded with additional nodes and edges, and you can query it using SPARQL to retrieve information.

Why Do Knowledge Graphs Matter?

Knowledge graphs provide a foundation for making sense of complex, interconnected data. They're used in search engines, recommendation systems, fraud detection, healthcare, and more. By connecting data points in a meaningful way, they help us answer questions, uncover insights, and even discover patterns we didn't know existed.

By understanding what a knowledge graph is and how it functions, you're taking the first step toward leveraging this powerful tool in your projects.

1.2 History and Evolution

The concept of knowledge graphs might seem like a modern innovation, but its roots run deep into the history of mathematics, computer science, and the web itself. To truly understand where knowledge graphs come from, it's important to trace their development step by step. This journey spans centuries, starting with foundational ideas in graph theory and evolving through the rise of semantic technologies and modern applications. Let's explore how these ideas matured into the powerful systems we use today.

Graph Theory

The story begins in 1736, when a mathematician named Leonhard Euler was presented with a puzzle involving the city of Königsberg. The city had seven bridges connecting its islands and riverbanks, and the challenge was to find a way to cross each bridge exactly once without retracing any steps. Euler realized that solving this problem wasn't about the physical bridges but the connections between the landmasses. He represented the landmasses as nodes and the bridges as edges, giving birth to graph theory.

Graph theory is the mathematical foundation of knowledge graphs. It formalized how relationships between entities could be represented as a network, enabling us to study not just individual elements but also the connections that bind them. Over the years, graph theory evolved and found applications in everything from transportation networks to social connections.

The Semantic Web Vision

In the 1990s, Tim Berners-Lee, the inventor of the World Wide Web, introduced the concept of the Semantic Web. His idea was simple yet profound: instead of the web being a collection of linked documents, what if it became a web of linked data? What if machines could understand the meaning of the information they processed, not just its structure?

To achieve this, Berners-Lee proposed several technologies:

- Resource Description Framework (RDF): A framework for representing information as triples (subject-predicate-object), such as "Paris is the capital of France."

- Web Ontology Language (OWL): A language for defining ontologies, which are formal descriptions of concepts and their relationships.

- SPARQL Protocol and RDF Query Language (SPARQL): A query language specifically designed for querying RDF data.

These technologies became the backbone of the Semantic Web. They provided a way to represent data as graphs, making relationships explicit and enabling machines to reason about the data.

```
Let's illustrate this with a simple RDF example.
Suppose we want to represent the fact that "Tim
Berners-Lee is the creator of the World Wide Web."
Here's how it looks in RDF:
@prefix ex: <http://example.org/> .
@prefix schema: <http://schema.org/> .

ex:TimBernersLee schema:creatorOf ex:WorldWideWeb .
```

This triple specifies:

- The subject: **Tim Berners-Lee**.
- The predicate: **creatorOf**.
- The object: **World Wide Web**.

The Semantic Web aimed to transform how data was linked and understood, laying the groundwork for modern knowledge graphs.

From Semantic Web to Knowledge Graphs

Despite its promise, the Semantic Web struggled to gain widespread adoption in its original form. The vision was ambitious, requiring global cooperation and adherence to standards, which proved challenging. However, the ideas behind the Semantic Web didn't fade; they evolved.

In 2012, Google introduced its **Knowledge Graph**, marking a pivotal moment in this evolution. Unlike the Semantic Web, which focused on creating an open web of linked data, Google's Knowledge Graph was built for a specific purpose: improving search. By connecting billions of entities—people, places, and things—and understanding their relationships, Google transformed search from a keyword-based system into one that understood meaning.

For instance, searching for "Leonardo da Vinci" would no longer return just a list of links. Instead, users would see a knowledge panel with information about him, his works, and related figures. This wasn't just data retrieval; it was knowledge representation.

Other companies followed suit, building their own knowledge graphs for various purposes:

- Facebook's **Social Graph** mapped relationships between people and their interests.
- Amazon used knowledge graphs to enhance product recommendations.
- Microsoft's **Satori** powered intelligent applications like Cortana and Bing.

These implementations weren't just about storing data; they were about making data **actionable** by understanding its meaning and context.

Real-World Example: Healthcare Knowledge Graphs

One of the most impactful applications of knowledge graphs has been in healthcare. Consider a system designed to assist doctors in diagnosing diseases. This system could use a knowledge graph to link:

- Symptoms (nodes) to diseases (nodes) via "is a symptom of" (edges).

- Diseases to treatments via "can be treated with."

- Treatments to side effects via "may cause."

Such a graph allows doctors to query the system in natural language, like "What diseases cause fever and rash?" or "What treatments are available for Type 2 diabetes?" The graph can not only retrieve relevant information but also infer new knowledge, such as identifying potential drug interactions based on shared pathways.

Exercise: Building a Historical Knowledge Graph

Let's create a small knowledge graph to represent historical figures and their achievements using Python and rdflib. This example captures connections between notable people and their contributions.

```python
from rdflib import Graph, URIRef, Literal,
Namespace, RDF

# Create a new graph
g = Graph()

# Define a namespace
EX = Namespace("http://example.org/")

# Add entities (nodes)
einstein = URIRef(EX.AlbertEinstein)
newton = URIRef(EX.IsaacNewton)
relativity = URIRef(EX.TheoryOfRelativity)
gravity = URIRef(EX.LawOfGravity)

# Add relationships (edges)
```

```
g.add((einstein, RDF.type, EX.Scientist))
g.add((newton, RDF.type, EX.Scientist))
g.add((einstein, EX.contributedTo, relativity))
g.add((newton, EX.contributedTo, gravity))

# Serialize the graph in Turtle format
print(g.serialize(format="turtle").decode("utf-8"))
```

When you run this code, the graph structure becomes clear. The nodes represent historical figures and concepts, and the edges define how they relate. Such graphs can be expanded with additional entities and relationships, eventually forming a comprehensive historical knowledge graph.

The Ongoing Evolution

Knowledge graphs continue to evolve, driven by advances in artificial intelligence and machine learning. Modern systems integrate graphs with natural language processing, enabling applications like chatbots and question-answering systems to understand context and deliver more accurate results. They also play a central role in explainable AI, providing transparent reasoning paths for decisions.

The journey from Euler's bridges to Google's Knowledge Graph illustrates how ideas grow and adapt over time. By combining the structure of graphs with the semantics of linked data, knowledge graphs have become indispensable tools for organizing and leveraging information in an interconnected world.

1.3 Why Knowledge Graphs Matter

Knowledge graphs are more than just a trendy buzzword in the technology space—they are a transformative way of organizing and understanding data. They don't simply store information; they connect it in meaningful ways, making it easier to interpret, analyze, and act upon. In this section, we'll explore why knowledge graphs are so important, not just in technical terms but in practical applications that influence businesses, governments, and individuals.

The Value of Connecting Information

To understand why knowledge graphs matter, consider how fragmented information can be. Data in organizations often exists in silos: customer data in one database, product data in another, and supplier data somewhere else. When information is disconnected like this, it becomes difficult to see the bigger picture. Knowledge graphs solve this problem by connecting disparate data sources and representing their relationships in a way that machines and humans can both understand.

For example, let's say a retail company wants to provide personalized recommendations to its customers. Using a traditional relational database, you could track customer purchases, but connecting those purchases to product metadata (like categories or reviews) and customer profiles becomes challenging. A knowledge graph can seamlessly connect customers, products, and reviews, enabling advanced recommendations.

This ability to connect and represent information contextually is what sets knowledge graphs apart. They allow us to not only query what exists but also infer new insights based on the relationships in the graph.

How Knowledge Graphs Enhance Decision-Making

At their core, knowledge graphs enable better decision-making. By organizing data into entities and relationships, they make it easier to analyze complex systems and draw conclusions. Let's take a real-world example to see this in action.

Healthcare Example:
A hospital uses a knowledge graph to link patient data, medical research, and treatment protocols. Here's how it works:

- The graph connects symptoms to diseases, diseases to treatments, and treatments to potential side effects.

- When a doctor inputs a patient's symptoms, the system can suggest potential diagnoses based on historical data and medical research.

- The graph can also highlight potential drug interactions, ensuring safer prescriptions.

This isn't just theoretical. Healthcare providers worldwide use knowledge graphs to power diagnostic tools, optimize patient care, and support medical research.

Here's how this might look in a simple knowledge graph structure:

- Nodes: Patient, Symptom, Disease, Treatment, Side Effect.

- Edges: "has symptom," "is associated with," "is treated by," "may cause."

This interconnected data allows doctors to ask nuanced questions like, "What treatments are available for diseases with symptoms X and Y that do not interact with drug Z?"

Improved Querying with Contextual Data

Traditional databases are excellent for structured queries but struggle with queries that require understanding context or relationships. Knowledge graphs shine in this area because they are inherently built for contextual queries. Let's demonstrate this with a practical example.

Suppose you're working for a library and want to recommend books based on user preferences. A traditional database query might look like this in SQL:

```
SELECT books.title
FROM books
JOIN categories ON books.category_id =
categories.id
JOIN authors ON books.author_id = authors.id
WHERE categories.name = 'Science Fiction'
AND authors.name = 'Isaac Asimov';
```

This works well if you have structured data in a fixed schema. But what if you want to add flexibility? For instance, what if you wanted to recommend books that are "related to" science fiction or "similar to" Isaac Asimov's works? Traditional databases struggle with such queries because they require dynamic relationships.

In a knowledge graph, the same query becomes simpler and more flexible:

```
PREFIX ex: <http://example.org/>

SELECT ?book
WHERE {
  ?book ex:category "Science Fiction" .
  ?book ex:author ex:IsaacAsimov .
}
```

Adding new relationships, like "related to" or "similar to," doesn't require restructuring the entire database. You can simply extend the graph schema and update the data.

Real-World Applications of Knowledge Graphs

Knowledge graphs have proven their value in various industries. Let's explore a few examples to see their impact.

Search Engines:
Google's Knowledge Graph, introduced in 2012, revolutionized how we search for information. When you search for "Leonardo da Vinci," you don't just get a list of links. Instead, you see a knowledge panel with his biography, works, and related figures. This is possible because Google organizes its data as a knowledge graph, connecting entities and their relationships.

E-Commerce:
Amazon uses knowledge graphs to recommend products. If you buy a smartphone, the system can recommend accessories like cases and chargers by understanding the relationships between products.

Finance:
Banks and financial institutions use knowledge graphs for fraud detection. By mapping transactions as a graph, they can identify unusual patterns, like a series of small withdrawals across accounts that are otherwise unconnected.

Education:
Online learning platforms use knowledge graphs to create personalized learning paths. A graph connects courses, topics, and prerequisites, enabling tailored recommendations based on a student's progress and goals.

Exercise: Building a Simple Knowledge Graph for Movie Recommendations

Let's create a small knowledge graph to represent movies, genres, and actors using Python and the rdflib library.

```python
from rdflib import Graph, URIRef, Literal, RDF,
Namespace

# Create a new graph
g = Graph()

# Define a namespace
EX = Namespace("http://example.org/")

# Add entities (nodes)
movie = URIRef(EX.Inception)
actor = URIRef(EX.LeonardoDiCaprio)
genre = URIRef(EX.ScienceFiction)

# Add relationships (edges)
g.add((movie, RDF.type, EX.Movie))
g.add((movie, EX.hasGenre, genre))
g.add((movie, EX.hasActor, actor))

# Serialize the graph in Turtle format
print(g.serialize(format="turtle").decode("utf-8"))
```

This code models a simple graph where the movie "Inception" is connected to its genre and lead actor. You can expand this graph with more movies, actors, and genres, creating a robust recommendation system.

Knowledge graphs matter because they transform how we organize, connect, and use information. They bring structure to complexity, enabling better decisions, smarter systems, and more personalized experiences. Whether you're building a search engine, optimizing healthcare, or developing a recommendation system, knowledge graphs provide the foundation for meaningful, actionable insights.

Their impact is already visible across industries, and as data continues to grow in volume and complexity, their importance will only increase. With the ability to bridge gaps between data silos, make sense of complex relationships, and support advanced queries, knowledge graphs are not just useful—they are essential.

Chapter 2: Core Concepts and Components

In this chapter, we'll explore the foundational ideas that make up knowledge graphs. These concepts are essential for understanding how knowledge graphs work and why they're so effective in representing complex data. Whether you're just starting out or looking to solidify your knowledge, this chapter will give you the essential tools to understand graph theory, key knowledge graph components, and the standards and frameworks that guide how graphs are built and queried.

2.1 Graph Basics

When we talk about knowledge graphs, we're fundamentally talking about graphs, a mathematical structure that allows us to model relationships between different entities. To truly grasp how knowledge graphs work, it's essential to first understand the basics of graph theory. Don't worry—this isn't a dry lecture on math. We'll approach it step by step and ensure it's practical, relevant, and easy to follow.

A graph is a way of representing relationships between things. It consists of two main components:

- **Nodes (or vertices):** These represent entities or objects.
- **Edges:** These represent the relationships between nodes.

Let's think of a real-world example: a social network. In this network:

- Each person is a **node**.
- A friendship between two people is an **edge** connecting the two nodes.

Graphs are incredibly versatile. They're not just limited to social networks but can represent almost any kind of relationship, whether it's between people, places, concepts, or even physical objects.

For example:

- In a transportation system, cities are nodes, and roads connecting them are edges.

- In a library catalog, books are nodes, and edges represent relationships like "written by" or "belongs to a genre."

Graphs are everywhere, and understanding them opens up a powerful way to model complex systems.

Key Properties of Graphs

There are some important concepts to understand about graphs, which will help you as we move forward.

1. **Directed vs. Undirected Graphs**
   In a directed graph, edges have a direction. For example, if we're modeling Twitter, where one user follows another, the edge would go from the follower to the person being followed. In contrast, an undirected graph doesn't have directional edges, like a Facebook friendship—it's mutual.

2. **Weighted vs. Unweighted Graphs**
   Edges can have weights to represent the strength or importance of a relationship. For instance, in a flight network, an edge between two cities could have a weight representing the distance or cost of the flight. In an unweighted graph, all edges are considered equal.

3. **Degree of a Node**
   The degree of a node is the number of edges connected to it. In a social network, the degree of a person's node would represent the number of friends or connections they have.

Graph Representation

Graphs can be represented in multiple ways, depending on the use case and computational efficiency.

Adjacency Matrix
An adjacency matrix is a two-dimensional array where each cell represents whether an edge exists between two nodes. If the graph is weighted, the cell contains the weight of the edge. For example:

```
 A B C

A 0 1 0

B 1 0 1

C 0 1 0
```

1.   Here, nodes A, B, and C are connected as indicated by 1s in the matrix.

Adjacency List
An adjacency list is a more memory-efficient way to represent a graph. It's essentially a dictionary where each key is a node, and the value is a list of connected nodes. For example:

```
{

    "A": ["B"],

    "B": ["A", "C"],

    "C": ["B"]

}
```

2.   The adjacency list is particularly useful for sparse graphs (graphs with relatively few edges compared to nodes) because it doesn't require storage for nonexistent edges.

Practical Example: Representing a Graph in Python

Let's build a simple graph in Python to see these concepts in action. Suppose we want to model a network of cities and roads connecting them.

```
# Using an adjacency list to represent the graph
graph = {
    "New York": ["Boston", "Chicago"],
    "Boston": ["New York", "Chicago"],
    "Chicago": ["New York", "Boston", "Denver"],
```

```
    "Denver": ["Chicago"]
}

# Printing the connections for each city
for city, connections in graph.items():
    print(f"{city} is connected to: {',
'.join(connections)}")
```

Output:

New York is connected to: Boston, Chicago

Boston is connected to: New York, Chicago

Chicago is connected to: New York, Boston, Denver

Denver is connected to: Chicago

Here, each city is a node, and the roads between cities are edges.

How Graphs Solve Real-World Problems

Graphs aren't just an academic exercise—they're incredibly practical. Let's explore a couple of real-world scenarios.

Social Networks:
When you think of platforms like Facebook, Instagram, or LinkedIn, you're thinking about graphs. Each user is a node, and their relationships—friends, followers, or connections—are edges. Graphs enable these platforms to recommend new connections ("People You May Know") by analyzing the relationships between nodes.

Search Engines:
Search engines like Google use graphs to model relationships between web pages. Each page is a node, and hyperlinks between them are edges. This graph helps determine the importance of a page (PageRank algorithm) and retrieve relevant results for your search query.

Exercise: Traversing a Graph

Graph traversal is the process of visiting all nodes in a graph to explore its structure or find specific information. There are two common algorithms for this:

- Breadth-First Search (BFS): Explores all neighbors of a node before moving to their neighbors.

- Depth-First Search (DFS): Explores as far as possible along a branch before backtracking.

Let's implement BFS in Python to find the shortest path between two nodes in our city network:

```python
from collections import deque

def bfs_shortest_path(graph, start, goal):
    # Keep track of visited nodes
    visited = set()
    # Use a queue to store paths
    queue = deque([[start]])

    while queue:
        # Get the first path from the queue
        path = queue.popleft()
        # Get the last node in the path
        node = path[-1]

        # Check if we've reached the goal
        if node == goal:
            return path

        # Skip visited nodes
        if node not in visited:
            visited.add(node)

            # Add paths to neighbors to the queue
            for neighbor in graph.get(node, []):
                new_path = list(path)
                new_path.append(neighbor)
                queue.append(new_path)

    return None
```

```
# Test the function
graph = {
    "New York": ["Boston", "Chicago"],
    "Boston": ["New York", "Chicago"],
    "Chicago": ["New York", "Boston", "Denver"],
    "Denver": ["Chicago"]
}

print(bfs_shortest_path(graph, "New York",
"Denver"))
```

Output:

['New York', 'Chicago', 'Denver']

This function demonstrates how graphs can be used to solve real-world problems like finding the shortest route between two locations.

Graphs are the foundation of knowledge graphs, providing a flexible and powerful way to model relationships between entities. Understanding graph basics—nodes, edges, properties like direction and weight, and methods for representation—is essential for building effective knowledge graphs. These principles aren't just theoretical; they're at the heart of practical applications in search engines, social networks, transportation systems, and more. With these foundational concepts in place, you're ready to explore the more advanced components of knowledge graphs.

2.2 Key Concepts in Knowledge Graphs

Now that you understand the basics of graph theory, let's discuss the unique concepts that make knowledge graphs so powerful. These concepts are what elevate graphs from a simple mathematical structure to a rich, meaningful way of representing and reasoning about knowledge. By the end of this section, you'll have a clear understanding of what makes knowledge graphs special and how these components come together to form systems that can store, query, and analyze complex information.

Entities: The Building Blocks of Knowledge Graphs

Every knowledge graph starts with **entities**. Entities are the "things" that the graph represents. These could be people, places, objects, events, or even abstract ideas. In technical terms, entities are often represented as **nodes** in the graph.

For example:

- A person like "Albert Einstein" is an entity.

- A place like "Paris" is an entity.

- A concept like "Relativity" is also an entity.

Each entity is unique and is typically identified using a Uniform Resource Identifier (URI). A URI acts as a global identifier for the entity, ensuring that it can be uniquely referenced across different systems. For instance:

- The entity "Albert Einstein" might have a URI like http://example.org/AlbertEinstein.

This unique identification is crucial because it allows different datasets to reference the same entity consistently, enabling integration and interoperability.

Relationships: Connecting the Dots

While entities are the building blocks, relationships are what give a knowledge graph its power. Relationships connect entities and define how they are related to one another. These are represented as **edges** in the graph.

For example:

- "Albert Einstein **developed** the Theory of Relativity."

- "Paris **is the capital of** France."

In this context:

- "developed" and "is the capital of" are the relationships.

- Relationships are often directional, meaning they have a starting point (subject) and an endpoint (object). For instance, in "Albert Einstein developed the Theory of Relativity," the direction flows from "Albert Einstein" to "Theory of Relativity."

Relationships can also have **types**, which describe the nature of the connection. In a well-structured knowledge graph, these relationship types are part of an **ontology** or schema that defines the valid connections between entities.

Attributes: Adding Context to Entities and Relationships

Entities and relationships often have additional information attached to them, known as **attributes** or **properties**. These attributes provide context and enrich the graph with detailed information.

For example:

- The entity "Albert Einstein" might have attributes like "birthdate: 1879-03-14" and "nationality: German."

- The relationship "developed" might have an attribute like "year: 1915" to indicate when Einstein developed the Theory of Relativity.

Attributes are key because they allow you to query and analyze the graph in more meaningful ways. For instance, you could ask, "Which scientists developed theories in the 20th century?" or "Find all capitals with populations greater than 1 million."

Ontology: The Structure of Knowledge

An ontology is a formal framework that defines the structure of a knowledge graph. It specifies:

1. The types of entities that exist (e.g., Person, Place, Event).

2. The types of relationships that can connect those entities (e.g., "works at," "is the capital of").

3. The attributes that entities and relationships can have.

Ontologies ensure consistency in how data is represented in the graph. They act as the "rules" of the graph, preventing invalid connections or attributes. For example:

- An ontology might specify that a "Person" can have a "birthdate" but not a "latitude."

- It might also define hierarchical relationships, such as "City" being a subclass of "Place."

A common standard for defining ontologies is the **Web Ontology Language (OWL)**, which allows for the creation of rich, semantic frameworks.

Inference: Discovering New Knowledge

One of the most exciting aspects of knowledge graphs is their ability to **infer** new knowledge from existing data. This is made possible by their structured nature and the semantics embedded in the ontology.

Let's take an example:

- Your graph knows that "Albert Einstein worked at Princeton University" and that "Princeton University is located in New Jersey."

- Even though the graph doesn't explicitly state it, you can infer that "Albert Einstein worked in New Jersey."

Inference is enabled by reasoning engines that apply logical rules to the graph. This makes knowledge graphs more than just data storage systems—they become systems of reasoning.

Querying Knowledge Graphs

To interact with and retrieve information from a knowledge graph, you use a query language. The most common one is **SPARQL (SPARQL Protocol and RDF Query Language)**. SPARQL allows you to write complex queries to extract data based on entities, relationships, and attributes.

Here's an example of a SPARQL query to find all scientists who developed theories:

```
PREFIX ex: <http://example.org/>

SELECT ?scientist ?theory
WHERE {
  ?scientist ex:developed ?theory .
  ?scientist rdf:type ex:Scientist .
}
```

This query:

- Looks for entities (?scientist) connected to theories (?theory) via the "developed" relationship.

- Filters entities that are of type "Scientist."

SPARQL is incredibly powerful, allowing you to ask nuanced questions like, "Find all theories developed before 1950 by German scientists."

Real-World Example: Knowledge Graph for Healthcare

In healthcare, a knowledge graph might connect patients, symptoms, diseases, and treatments. Here's a simplified example:

- Entities: "John Doe" (Patient), "Fever" (Symptom), "Influenza" (Disease), "Antiviral Drug" (Treatment).

- Relationships:

  - "John Doe has Symptom Fever."

  - "Fever is associated with Influenza."

  - "Influenza is treated by Antiviral Drug."

With this graph, a doctor could query, "What treatments are available for patients with Fever?" The graph could even infer possible diseases based on symptoms.

Here's a Python example using the rdflib library to represent this:

```python
from rdflib import Graph, URIRef, Literal, RDF,
Namespace

# Create a new graph
g = Graph()

# Define a namespace
EX = Namespace("http://example.org/")

# Add entities and relationships
john = URIRef(EX.JohnDoe)
fever = URIRef(EX.Fever)
influenza = URIRef(EX.Influenza)
antiviral = URIRef(EX.AntiviralDrug)
```

```
g.add((john, EX.hasSymptom, fever))
g.add((fever, EX.associatedWith, influenza))
g.add((influenza, EX.treatedBy, antiviral))

# Serialize the graph in Turtle format
print(g.serialize(format="turtle").decode("utf-8"))
```

Output:

@prefix ex: <http://example.org/> .

ex:JohnDoe ex:hasSymptom ex:Fever .

ex:Fever ex:associatedWith ex:Influenza .

ex:Influenza ex:treatedBy ex:AntiviralDrug .

With this graph, you could query:

- "What diseases are associated with Fever?"
- "What treatments are available for Influenza?"

The key concepts in knowledge graphs—entities, relationships, attributes, ontology, inference, and querying—are what make them so versatile and powerful. These components allow knowledge graphs to not only represent complex systems but also reason about them and extract meaningful insights. As you continue learning, these foundational concepts will be your guide to understanding how knowledge graphs are built and applied in real-world scenarios.

2.3 Standards and Frameworks

Standards and frameworks are the backbone of any knowledge graph. They ensure consistency, interoperability, and scalability, allowing knowledge graphs to work seamlessly across different systems, tools, and applications. Without these standards, each organization or developer might implement knowledge graphs in entirely different ways, making it difficult to share, integrate, or query data effectively.

In this section, we'll discuss the essential standards and frameworks that power knowledge graphs. We'll look at how they define the structure, semantics, and interactions within a graph, and we'll also work through practical examples to show how these standards are applied.

The Role of Standards in Knowledge Graphs

Standards in knowledge graphs serve several key purposes:

1. Uniformity: They provide a common language for describing entities, relationships, and data structures.

2. Interoperability: They enable systems to integrate and share data without confusion.

3. Scalability: They allow graphs to grow and evolve without breaking existing structures.

4. Reasoning: They enable logical inference by providing clear semantics and rules.

Think of standards as the grammar and syntax of a language. Just as grammar ensures that sentences make sense, standards ensure that a knowledge graph is meaningful and machine-readable.

RDF: Resource Description Framework

The Resource Description Framework (RDF) is one of the most fundamental standards for building knowledge graphs. RDF is a framework for representing data as **triples**, where each triple consists of three parts:

1. **Subject:** The entity you're describing.

2. **Predicate:** The property or relationship.

3. **Object:** The value or entity connected to the subject.

For example, if you want to represent "Albert Einstein was born in Ulm," the RDF triple would look like this:

- Subject: Albert Einstein

- Predicate: was born in

- Object: Ulm

RDF is versatile because it represents data in a graph-like structure, making it ideal for knowledge graphs.

Here's how you might write this triple in RDF's **Turtle format**, a human-readable syntax:

```
@prefix ex: <http://example.org/> .

ex:AlbertEinstein ex:bornIn ex:Ulm .
```

This simple syntax defines:

- A prefix (ex:) for your namespace.

- The relationship between the subject (ex:AlbertEinstein), predicate (ex:bornIn), and object (ex:Ulm).

RDF triples can be stored and queried efficiently, making RDF a cornerstone of knowledge graph standards.

OWL: Web Ontology Language

The Web Ontology Language (OWL) builds on RDF by providing a way to define complex relationships, hierarchies, and constraints in a knowledge graph. While RDF is excellent for storing data, OWL enables reasoning and inference by defining rules and semantics.

OWL is used to create **ontologies**, which are structured frameworks that define:

- **Classes:** Categories or types of entities (e.g., Person, City).

- **Properties:** Attributes or relationships (e.g., "born in," "is a capital of").

- **Constraints:** Rules about relationships (e.g., "A person can only have one birth date").

For instance, in a geographic knowledge graph, you might use OWL to define:

- A "City" is a subclass of "Place."

- A "Country" can have multiple "Cities," but each "City" belongs to only one "Country."

Here's an example of an OWL ontology written in Turtle syntax:

```
@prefix ex: <http://example.org/> .
@prefix rdf: <http://www.w3.org/1999/02/22-rdf-
syntax-ns#> .
@prefix owl: <http://www.w3.org/2002/07/owl#> .

ex:City rdf:type owl:Class .
ex:Country rdf:type owl:Class .
ex:hasCapital rdf:type owl:ObjectProperty ;
              owl:domain ex:Country ;
              owl:range ex:City .
```

This ontology defines:

- Two classes: City and Country.

- A property, hasCapital, that links a Country to a City.

With OWL, reasoning engines can infer new knowledge. For example, if "Paris is the capital of France" and "France is a country," the engine can infer that "Paris is a city."

SPARQL: Querying Knowledge Graphs

SPARQL (SPARQL Protocol and RDF Query Language) is the standard language for querying RDF data. It's like SQL but designed specifically for graphs. With SPARQL, you can extract information from a knowledge graph, even if the data spans multiple relationships.

Let's look at a simple SPARQL query. Suppose you have a graph of scientists and their discoveries, and you want to find all discoveries made by Albert Einstein:

```
PREFIX ex: <http://example.org/>

SELECT ?discovery
WHERE {
  ex:AlbertEinstein ex:discovered ?discovery .
}
```

This query asks the graph to find all ?discovery values connected to ex:AlbertEinstein via the ex:discovered relationship.

Here's how a small RDF dataset for this query might look:

```
@prefix ex: <http://example.org/> .

ex:AlbertEinstein ex:discovered
ex:TheoryOfRelativity .
ex:AlbertEinstein ex:discovered
ex:PhotoelectricEffect .
```

The query would return:

discovery

ex:TheoryOfRelativity

ex:PhotoelectricEffect

SPARQL's ability to handle relationships and infer connections makes it indispensable for working with knowledge graphs.

Real-World Applications of Standards

Standards like RDF, OWL, and SPARQL are used across industries to build robust and interoperable knowledge graphs. Let's look at a real-world example to see how these standards come together.

Google Knowledge Graph:
Google uses RDF-like structures to connect billions of entities—people, places, things—and their relationships. When you search for "Barack Obama," Google's Knowledge Graph can show you:

- Related entities like Michelle Obama or Joe Biden.

- Attributes like his birthdate, presidency, and books authored.

This seamless integration is powered by adherence to semantic web standards, allowing Google to integrate and reason about vast amounts of data.

Healthcare Knowledge Graphs:
In healthcare, knowledge graphs connect diseases, symptoms, treatments, and patients. Using OWL, a hospital might define:

- "Diabetes" as a subclass of "Chronic Disease."

- A "Treatment" property linking diseases to their medications.

With SPARQL, doctors could query, "What treatments are available for chronic diseases?" The system could infer connections between related diseases and treatments, even if the exact match isn't explicitly stored.

Exercise: Building and Querying a Simple Knowledge Graph

Let's create and query a knowledge graph using Python and the rdflib library.

Step 1: Create the Graph

```python
from rdflib import Graph, URIRef, Namespace, Literal

# Define a namespace
EX = Namespace("http://example.org/")

# Create a graph
g = Graph()

# Add triples
g.add((EX.AlbertEinstein, EX.discovered, EX.TheoryOfRelativity))
g.add((EX.AlbertEinstein, EX.discovered, EX.PhotoelectricEffect))
g.add((EX.TheoryOfRelativity, EX.field, EX.Physics))

# Save the graph
print(g.serialize(format="turtle").decode("utf-8"))

Step 2: Query the Graph
from rdflib.plugins.sparql import prepareQuery

# Define the query
query = prepareQuery(
    """
    PREFIX ex: <http://example.org/>
    SELECT ?discovery
    WHERE {
        ex:AlbertEinstein ex:discovered ?discovery
```

```
        }
        """ """
)

# Execute the query
for row in g.query(query):
    print(f"Discovery: {row.discovery}")
```

Output:

Discovery: http://example.org/TheoryOfRelativity

Discovery: http://example.org/PhotoelectricEffect

Standards and frameworks like RDF, OWL, and SPARQL form the backbone of knowledge graphs, ensuring that data is consistent, meaningful, and interoperable. They allow developers to build systems that are not just storage solutions but tools for reasoning and discovery. Understanding these standards is critical for anyone looking to create or work with knowledge graphs, as they unlock the full potential of graph-based systems.

Chapter 3: Designing Knowledge Graphs

Designing a knowledge graph is a thoughtful process that requires a clear understanding of the data, its relationships, and the goals you aim to achieve. It's more than just connecting nodes and edges—it's about creating a structured, meaningful, and scalable representation of information. In this chapter, we'll explore the design process step by step, starting with planning and requirements, followed by ontology design, and finally graph modeling.

3.1 Planning and Requirements

Designing a knowledge graph begins with understanding what you want to achieve and why it's needed. Planning and defining requirements is one of the most important steps because it sets the foundation for everything that follows. If you start with a clear purpose and a well-defined scope, the rest of the process becomes much smoother. Let's work through the essential aspects of planning and requirements together.

Understanding the Problem

Before you even think about nodes, edges, or data, you need to understand the problem your knowledge graph is meant to solve. What are you trying to achieve? Who will use it, and how will it help them? These are fundamental questions that shape your design.

For example, let's say you're working with a university library. They want a system that connects books, authors, research topics, and student interests. The problem they face is that their current system treats everything as isolated data. Students can't easily discover books related to their courses or find connections between different topics.

The knowledge graph you design for this case should solve these challenges by representing entities like "Books," "Authors," "Courses," and "Topics," and linking them meaningfully. By identifying the problem clearly, you've already taken the first step toward a useful solution.

Defining Your Audience and Stakeholders

Knowing who will use your knowledge graph helps you tailor its design to their needs. In the example of the university library, the audience includes:

- Students searching for books and topics.

- Librarians managing book metadata.

- Researchers exploring interdisciplinary connections.

Stakeholders might also include IT teams who will maintain the graph or university administrators who want reports on library usage patterns.

Each of these groups has different priorities. Students care about easy-to-use search tools, while IT teams need the graph to integrate with existing systems. Understanding these perspectives ensures your knowledge graph serves everyone effectively.

Identifying and Gathering Data

Once you understand the problem and your audience, the next step is to identify where your data will come from. A knowledge graph is only as good as the data it contains, so this is a critical part of planning.

Start by listing all potential data sources. These could include:

- **Structured data:** Databases, CSV files, or APIs.

- **Semi-structured data:** XML or JSON files.

- **Unstructured data:** Text documents, emails, or web pages.

For the library example, structured data might come from their existing catalog system, while unstructured data could include research papers or book reviews.

Let's consider an e-commerce use case. If you're building a knowledge graph to improve product recommendations, your data might come from:

- Customer profiles.

- Product catalogs with metadata like categories and prices.

- Purchase history.

Here's a simple code example of how you might load product data into a graph in Python:

```python
from rdflib import Graph, URIRef, Literal,
Namespace, RDF

# Define a namespace
EX = Namespace("http://example.org/")

# Create a new graph
g = Graph()

# Add product data
product = URIRef(EX.Product1)
category = URIRef(EX.Electronics)
g.add((product, RDF.type, EX.Product))
g.add((product, EX.hasName, Literal("Smartphone")))
g.add((product, EX.belongsToCategory, category))

# Serialize the graph to view the data
print(g.serialize(format="turtle").decode("utf-8"))

Output:
@prefix ex: <http://example.org/> .

ex:Product1 rdf:type ex:Product ;
            ex:hasName "Smartphone" ;
            ex:belongsToCategory ex:Electronics .
```

In this snippet, you've already structured the data in a way that makes it easy to query and analyze later.

Defining the Scope

It's tempting to include everything in your knowledge graph, but that's often a mistake, especially when starting out. A focused scope makes the project manageable and ensures that the graph is useful from the beginning.

Think about what's essential for your use case. For the university library, you might initially focus on books, authors, and research topics. Once you've built and tested that graph, you could expand it to include student interests or library events.

Scoping also involves defining the **depth** of your graph. For example:

- Do you need to represent detailed relationships between entities, like "co-authored with" or "translated by" for books?

- Or is a simpler model, like "written by," enough for now?

Defining the scope prevents you from over-complicating the graph and ensures that your project stays on track.

Establishing Goals and Success Metrics

A clear definition of success keeps your project focused and helps you evaluate whether your knowledge graph is achieving its intended purpose. Goals might include:

- Improving the accuracy of search results.

- Reducing the time it takes to answer specific queries.

- Enabling new types of insights, like identifying patterns in research topics.

For each goal, define measurable metrics. For example:

- **Query performance:** Average time to return a search result.

- **Coverage:** Percentage of books in the catalog linked to at least one author and topic.

- **User satisfaction:** Survey results from students and librarians.

These metrics provide a way to measure progress and identify areas for improvement.

Tools and Technologies

Part of planning involves deciding which tools and technologies you'll use to build your graph. Here are some considerations:

- Graph databases: Will you use Neo4j, Amazon Neptune, or another platform?

- Standards and frameworks: Will you use RDF, OWL, or property graphs?

- Integration tools: Do you need ETL tools to transform and load data?

For the library example, you might choose a graph database like Neo4j for its visualization capabilities and use RDF as the standard for data representation.

Here's a simple Neo4j query to create and link entities for the library use case:

```
CREATE (b:Book {title: "Knowledge Graphs 101"})
CREATE (a:Author {name: "John Doe"})
CREATE (b)-[:WRITTEN_BY]->(a)
```

This query creates a book node, an author node, and a "WRITTEN_BY" relationship between them. Tools like Neo4j make it easy to visualize and query this data.

Challenges and Risks

No project is without challenges. Identifying potential risks early helps you prepare for them. Common challenges include:

- Data quality: Inconsistent or incomplete data can lead to errors in the graph.

- Scalability: As your graph grows, can your infrastructure handle the load?

- Integration: Will the graph work seamlessly with existing systems?

For each challenge, plan a mitigation strategy. For example, if data quality is a concern, implement a data cleaning process during the ETL phase.

Real-World Example: Planning a Healthcare Knowledge Graph

Let's consider a healthcare knowledge graph aimed at connecting patients, symptoms, diseases, and treatments. During planning, you might:

1. Identify the use case: Help doctors diagnose diseases more accurately.

2. Define the audience: Doctors and medical researchers.

3. Gather data: Electronic health records, medical textbooks, and clinical guidelines.

4. Scope the project: Start with common diseases and their symptoms.

5. Set goals: Reduce diagnosis errors by 10% and improve query response times.

With a clear plan, you can design a graph that meets these needs, starting small and expanding as you gain insights and feedback.

Planning and defining requirements is the cornerstone of designing an effective knowledge graph. By understanding the problem, identifying your audience, gathering data, and defining a clear scope and goals, you set yourself up for success. A well-planned knowledge graph not only solves specific problems but also becomes a foundation for future growth and innovation. With this approach, you're ready to move into the next step: designing the ontology that will structure your graph.

3.2 Ontology Design

Ontology design is the foundation of a well-structured knowledge graph. It's about defining the framework that describes the entities in your graph, their relationships, and the rules that govern their interactions. A good ontology ensures your knowledge graph is meaningful, consistent, and scalable. In this section, I'll guide you through the process of designing an ontology, explaining each concept in detail and showing you how to implement it step by step.

An ontology is essentially a blueprint for your knowledge graph. It defines:

1. Classes (Types): Categories of entities, like "Person," "City," or "Book."

2. Relationships (Properties): How these entities connect, such as "lives in" or "written by."

3. Attributes (Data Properties): Characteristics of entities, like "name," "age," or "title."

4. Rules and Constraints: Logic that defines how entities and relationships behave, such as "A book must have at least one author."

Think of an ontology as a guide that ensures your graph is meaningful and logical. Without it, your graph might end up being just a collection of disconnected data points.

Steps to Designing an Ontology

1. Identify Key Concepts

The first step is to identify the key concepts relevant to your use case. These concepts will become the classes in your ontology. Let's take the example of an e-commerce knowledge graph. Here, the key concepts might include:

- **Product**

- **Customer**

- **Order**

- **Category**

Each concept represents a category of entities that will appear in your graph.

2. Define Relationships

Once you have your classes, think about how they are connected. Relationships are the backbone of your knowledge graph—they define how entities interact. In the e-commerce example:

- A Customer "places" an Order.

- An Order "contains" a Product.

- A Product "belongs to" a Category.

Relationships should be meaningful and relevant to your use case. Avoid creating overly generic or redundant relationships.

3. Add Attributes

Attributes provide additional details about entities and relationships. For instance:

- A Customer might have attributes like name, email, and address.

- A Product might have attributes like price, brand, and stock level.

These attributes make your graph richer and enable more detailed queries.

4. Define Rules and Constraints

Rules and constraints ensure your ontology reflects real-world logic. For example:

- A Product must belong to at least one Category.

- An Order must have at least one Product.

You can also define cardinality constraints, such as:

- A Customer can place multiple Orders, but an Order can only be placed by one Customer.

Using Standards for Ontology Design

Standards like **OWL (Web Ontology Language)** make it easier to define and share ontologies. OWL provides tools to specify classes, relationships, and constraints in a formal, machine-readable format.

Here's a simple ontology for our e-commerce example in OWL, using Turtle syntax:

```
@prefix ex: <http://example.org/> .
@prefix rdf: <http://www.w3.org/1999/02/22-rdf-
syntax-ns#> .
@prefix rdfs: <http://www.w3.org/2000/01/rdf-
schema#> .
```

```
@prefix owl: <http://www.w3.org/2002/07/owl#> .

# Define Classes
ex:Product rdf:type owl:Class .
ex:Customer rdf:type owl:Class .
ex:Order rdf:type owl:Class .
ex:Category rdf:type owl:Class .

# Define Relationships
ex:places rdf:type owl:ObjectProperty ;
          rdfs:domain ex:Customer ;
          rdfs:range ex:Order .

ex:contains rdf:type owl:ObjectProperty ;
            rdfs:domain ex:Order ;
            rdfs:range ex:Product .

ex:belongsToCategory rdf:type owl:ObjectProperty ;
                     rdfs:domain ex:Product ;
                     rdfs:range ex:Category .
```

This ontology defines:

- Four classes (Product, Customer, Order, Category).

- Three relationships (places, contains, belongsToCategory) with their domains (starting points) and ranges (endpoints).

Building the Ontology in Practice

Let's implement this ontology using Python and the rdflib library.

Step 1: Define Classes and Relationships

```
from rdflib import Graph, URIRef, Namespace, RDF

# Define namespaces
EX = Namespace("http://example.org/")

# Create a graph
g = Graph()

# Define classes
g.add((EX.Product, RDF.type, RDF.Class))
```

```
g.add((EX.Customer, RDF.type, RDF.Class))
g.add((EX.Order, RDF.type, RDF.Class))
g.add((EX.Category, RDF.type, RDF.Class))

# Define relationships
g.add((EX.places, RDF.type, RDF.Property))
g.add((EX.places, RDF.domain, EX.Customer))
g.add((EX.places, RDF.range, EX.Order))

g.add((EX.contains, RDF.type, RDF.Property))
g.add((EX.contains, RDF.domain, EX.Order))
g.add((EX.contains, RDF.range, EX.Product))

g.add((EX.belongsToCategory, RDF.type,
RDF.Property))
g.add((EX.belongsToCategory, RDF.domain,
EX.Product))
g.add((EX.belongsToCategory, RDF.range,
EX.Category))

# Serialize the graph to view it
print(g.serialize(format="turtle").decode("utf-8"))
```

Output:

```
@prefix ex: <http://example.org/> .

ex:Product rdf:type rdf:Class .
ex:Customer rdf:type rdf:Class .
ex:Order rdf:type rdf:Class .
ex:Category rdf:type rdf:Class .

ex:places rdf:type rdf:Property ;
        rdf:domain ex:Customer ;
        rdf:range ex:Order .

ex:contains rdf:type rdf:Property ;
        rdf:domain ex:Order ;
        rdf:range ex:Product .

ex:belongsToCategory rdf:type rdf:Property ;
                rdf:domain ex:Product ;
                rdf:range ex:Category .
```

Step 2: Add Entities and Relationships

```python
# Add entities
customer = URIRef(EX.Customer1)
order = URIRef(EX.Order1)
product = URIRef(EX.Product1)
category = URIRef(EX.Category1)

# Add relationships
g.add((customer, RDF.type, EX.Customer))
g.add((order, RDF.type, EX.Order))
g.add((product, RDF.type, EX.Product))
g.add((category, RDF.type, EX.Category))

g.add((customer, EX.places, order))
g.add((order, EX.contains, product))
g.add((product, EX.belongsToCategory, category))

# Serialize the graph to view it
print(g.serialize(format="turtle").decode("utf-8"))
```

```
Output:
@prefix ex: <http://example.org/> .

ex:Customer1 rdf:type ex:Customer ;
             ex:places ex:Order1 .

ex:Order1 rdf:type ex:Order ;
          ex:contains ex:Product1 .

ex:Product1 rdf:type ex:Product ;
            ex:belongsToCategory ex:Category1 .

ex:Category1 rdf:type ex:Category .
```

This expanded graph now includes actual data, connecting a customer to an order, a product, and its category.

Testing and Refining the Ontology

Ontology design is an iterative process. Once you've built your initial model, test it by running queries to ensure it meets your needs. For instance, using SPARQL, you could query:

- "What products belong to a given category?"

- "Which customers have placed orders?"

Refine your ontology based on feedback and new requirements. A good ontology evolves over time as your knowledge graph grows.

Ontology design is the heart of knowledge graph creation. By carefully defining classes, relationships, attributes, and rules, you create a framework that ensures your graph is consistent, meaningful, and useful. Whether you're building a graph for e-commerce, healthcare, or any other domain, a well-designed ontology is the foundation for success. By following these principles and practices, you'll be able to design ontologies that not only meet current needs but also adapt to future challenges.

3.3 Graph Modeling

Graph modeling is the process of structuring your data into a graph that reflects real-world entities and their relationships in a meaningful and efficient way. Think of graph modeling as turning your conceptual framework—your ontology—into a practical, working graph. This step bridges the gap between theory and implementation, ensuring your knowledge graph is ready to be populated, queried, and expanded.

Graph modeling involves creating a structure for your knowledge graph that represents:

1. **Entities (Nodes):** The "things" in your graph, such as people, places, or products.

2. **Relationships (Edges):** The connections between entities, which define how they interact.

3. **Attributes (Properties):** The details about entities and relationships, such as names, dates, or measurements.

Graph modeling is all about ensuring that these elements are represented in a way that aligns with the real-world scenario you're modeling while keeping the graph intuitive, scalable, and efficient for queries.

Steps in Graph Modeling

1. Understand the Data and Use Case

The first step in graph modeling is to understand the data you're working with and how it relates to the problem you're solving. Ask yourself:

- What entities are most important for the use case?
- How are these entities connected in the real world?
- What details about these entities and relationships are relevant?

Let's consider a movie recommendation system as an example. The key entities might be:

- Movies
- Actors
- Directors
- Genres
- Users

The relationships could include:

- "acted in" (Actor → Movie)
- "directed by" (Movie → Director)
- "belongs to" (Movie → Genre)
- "rated" (User → Movie)

The details might include:

- Attributes for movies (e.g., title, release year, rating).
- Attributes for users (e.g., username, preferences).

- Properties for relationships (e.g., rating score for "rated").

Understanding these aspects will guide your graph modeling.

2. Define the Schema

A schema defines the structure of your graph. It specifies:

- **Node types:** The categories of entities (e.g., Movie, Actor, User).

- **Edge types:** The types of relationships (e.g., "acted in," "rated").

- **Attributes:** The properties of nodes and edges (e.g., a movie's title, a user's rating score).

For our movie example, the schema might look like this:

- **Nodes:**
    - Movie: Attributes = {title, releaseYear, averageRating}
    - User: Attributes = {username, age, preferences}
    - Actor: Attributes = {name, birthdate}
    - Director: Attributes = {name, birthdate}

- **Edges:**
    - "acted in": Between Actor and Movie
    - "directed by": Between Director and Movie
    - "rated": Between User and Movie, with an attribute ratingScore

3. Create the Graph Model

Once the schema is defined, you can build the graph model. This involves creating nodes for each entity, edges for relationships, and assigning attributes.

Here's an example in Python using the networkx library, which is a popular tool for working with graphs:

```python
import networkx as nx

# Create a directed graph
graph = nx.DiGraph()

# Add nodes with attributes
graph.add_node("Inception", type="Movie",
releaseYear=2010, averageRating=8.8)
graph.add_node("Leonardo DiCaprio", type="Actor",
birthdate="1974-11-11")
graph.add_node("Christopher Nolan",
type="Director", birthdate="1970-07-30")
graph.add_node("User1", type="User",
username="johndoe", preferences="Sci-Fi")

# Add edges with attributes
graph.add_edge("Leonardo DiCaprio", "Inception",
relationship="acted in")
graph.add_edge("Christopher Nolan", "Inception",
relationship="directed by")
graph.add_edge("User1", "Inception",
relationship="rated", ratingScore=5)

# Print the graph
print(graph.nodes(data=True))
print(graph.edges(data=True))
```

Output:

[('Inception', {'type': 'Movie', 'releaseYear': 2010, 'averageRating': 8.8}),

('Leonardo DiCaprio', {'type': 'Actor', 'birthdate': '1974-11-11'}),

('Christopher Nolan', {'type': 'Director', 'birthdate': '1970-07-30'}),

('User1', {'type': 'User', 'username': 'johndoe', 'preferences': 'Sci-Fi'})]

[('Leonardo DiCaprio', 'Inception', {'relationship': 'acted in'}),

('Christopher Nolan', 'Inception', {'relationship': 'directed by'}),

('User1', 'Inception', {'relationship': 'rated', 'ratingScore': 5})]

This snippet models a simple graph with movies, users, actors, and directors. It shows how nodes and edges can be enriched with attributes.

4. Optimize the Model

As your graph grows, optimization becomes essential to ensure performance and scalability. Here are some strategies:

- **Use indexing:** Index frequently queried attributes to speed up searches.

- **Avoid redundant relationships:** Only include relationships that add value to the graph.

- **Normalize attributes:** Use consistent naming conventions and data formats.

For example, instead of storing a user's age as an attribute, store their birthdate and calculate age dynamically.

5. Test the Graph

Testing is a crucial step in graph modeling. Run queries to ensure the graph is structured correctly and provides the expected results. For example, using a graph database like Neo4j, you might query:

- "Find all movies directed by Christopher Nolan."

- "List all users who rated Inception."

Here's how a query might look in Neo4j's Cypher query language:

```
MATCH (m:Movie)-[:DIRECTED_BY]->(d:Director)
WHERE d.name = "Christopher Nolan"
RETURN m.title
```

This query retrieves all movies directed by Christopher Nolan.

Real-World Example: Social Network Graph

Let's model a social network. In this graph:

- **Nodes:** Users

- **Edges:** Relationships like "friends with" and "follows"
- **Attributes:** User details (e.g., name, location, interests)

Here's how it might look in Python:

```python
# Create the graph
social_graph = nx.Graph()

# Add nodes
social_graph.add_node("Alice", type="User",
location="New York", interests=["Tech", "Books"])
social_graph.add_node("Bob", type="User",
location="San Francisco", interests=["Music",
"Tech"])

# Add edges
social_graph.add_edge("Alice", "Bob",
relationship="friends with")

# Query the graph
for user, data in social_graph.nodes(data=True):
    print(f"{user} ({data['location']}) is
interested in {', '.join(data['interests'])}.")
```

Output:

Alice (New York) is interested in Tech, Books.

Bob (San Francisco) is interested in Music, Tech.

This graph could be expanded to include more users, additional relationships (e.g., "follows"), and richer attributes.

Common Pitfalls in Graph Modeling

- Overcomplicating the Schema: Including too many node types or relationships can make the graph hard to use and maintain. Start simple and expand as needed.

- Ignoring Query Requirements: Design your graph with queries in mind. If a common query involves finding movies by genre, ensure the "belongs to" relationship is included.

- Lack of Validation: Regularly validate the graph against your schema to ensure data consistency.

Graph modeling is the bridge between your conceptual ontology and a working knowledge graph. By understanding your data, defining a clear schema, and implementing it with tools like networkx or Neo4j, you can create a graph that is both functional and scalable. With careful testing and optimization, your graph will not only represent the real world accurately but also empower powerful queries and insights.

Chapter 4: Building and Implementing Knowledge Graphs

Designing a knowledge graph is only the beginning. The real challenge lies in building and implementing it effectively. This chapter takes you through the process of integrating and preparing data, selecting the right platforms and tools, and learning how to query and reason with your knowledge graph. By the end, you'll have a comprehensive understanding of how to turn your design into a working system that delivers meaningful insights.

4.1 Data Integration and Preparation

Data integration and preparation are critical steps in building a knowledge graph. These steps ensure that your graph accurately represents real-world entities and their relationships. Without clean, well-structured, and well-connected data, your knowledge graph won't deliver the insights or functionality you need.

Data integration is the process of collecting and combining data from multiple sources into a single, unified graph. Knowledge graphs often rely on diverse datasets, such as relational databases, APIs, spreadsheets, and even unstructured text like research articles or social media posts. Integrating these data sources ensures that all relevant information is represented and connected.

Let's consider an example. Suppose you're building a knowledge graph for a healthcare organization. You might integrate:

1. Patient records from a database.

2. Clinical trial results in JSON format.

3. Research papers in plain text.

Each of these sources is valuable but presents its own challenges in terms of structure, format, and quality. Integration involves addressing these challenges to create a seamless, unified graph.

Understanding Data Sources

Before integrating data, you need to analyze your sources. Here's how you can approach this step:

1. **Structured Data**
   Structured data is already organized into tables, rows, and columns. For example:

   - Relational databases like MySQL or PostgreSQL.

   - Spreadsheets (CSV or Excel files).

These sources are relatively straightforward to work with because their schema is explicit.

2. **Semi-Structured Data**
   Semi-structured data includes formats like XML and JSON, where the structure is flexible. For instance:

   - A JSON file with nested fields describing products and categories.

   - An XML file with metadata about research papers.

This data often requires parsing and flattening to align with your graph schema.

3. **Unstructured Data**
   Unstructured data lacks a predefined format. Examples include:

   - Text documents, such as PDFs or Word files.

   - Social media posts or emails.

For these sources, you'll need natural language processing (NLP) tools to extract entities and relationships.

Data Preparation

Once you've identified your data sources, the next step is to clean, transform, and prepare the data for your graph. This process is often referred to as **ETL (Extract, Transform, Load).**

1. Extract

The extraction step involves retrieving data from its source. The method depends on the type of source:

- For relational databases, you can use SQL queries to extract the relevant data.

- For APIs, you'll use HTTP requests to fetch data in JSON or XML format.

- For unstructured text, tools like Apache Tika can extract plain text from documents.

Here's an example of extracting data from a relational database using Python and pymysql:

```python
import pymysql
import pandas as pd

# Connect to the database
connection = pymysql.connect(
    host='localhost',
    user='root',
    password='password',
    database='healthcare'
)

# Query the data
query = "SELECT * FROM patients;"
patients_df = pd.read_sql(query, connection)

# Close the connection
connection.close()

# Display the data
print(patients_df.head())
```

This script retrieves patient data from a MySQL database and stores it in a Pandas DataFrame for further processing.

2. Transform

The transformation step involves cleaning and restructuring the data to fit your knowledge graph's schema. Common transformation tasks include:

- **Standardizing formats:** Converting dates to a consistent format (YYYY-MM-DD).

- **Resolving duplicates:** Merging duplicate records based on unique identifiers.

- **Mapping to ontology:** Aligning data fields with the classes and properties in your ontology.

For instance, if your ontology defines a "Patient" class with attributes like "name," "age," and "disease," you'll map the columns from your database to these attributes.

Here's an example of transforming a dataset:

```python
# Standardize date formats
patients_df['date_of_birth'] =
pd.to_datetime(patients_df['date_of_birth']).dt.str
ftime('%Y-%m-%d')

# Map columns to ontology attributes
patients_df.rename(columns={
    'full_name': 'name',
    'age_years': 'age',
    'diagnosis': 'disease'
}, inplace=True)

# Display the transformed data
print(patients_df.head())
```

This snippet standardizes date formats and renames columns to match the ontology.

3. Load

The loading step involves populating your knowledge graph with the cleaned and transformed data. If you're working with an RDF-based graph, you'll represent the data as triples (subject, predicate, object).

Here's an example using rdflib to load patient data into an RDF graph:

```python
from rdflib import Graph, URIRef, Literal,
Namespace, RDF

# Define namespaces
EX = Namespace("http://example.org/")
```

```
# Create a graph
g = Graph()

# Add patient data
for _, row in patients_df.iterrows():
    patient = URIRef(EX[row['id']])
    g.add((patient, RDF.type, EX.Patient))
    g.add((patient, EX.hasName,
Literal(row['name'])))
    g.add((patient, EX.hasAge,
Literal(row['age'])))
    g.add((patient, EX.hasDisease,
Literal(row['disease'])))

# Serialize the graph
print(g.serialize(format="turtle").decode("utf-8"))
```

Output:

@prefix ex: <http://example.org/> .

ex:1 rdf:type ex:Patient ;

    ex:hasName "John Doe" ;

    ex:hasAge 45 ;

    ex:hasDisease "Diabetes" .

ex:2 rdf:type ex:Patient ;

    ex:hasName "Jane Smith" ;

    ex:hasAge 34 ;

    ex:hasDisease "Hypertension" .

This output represents patient data as RDF triples, ready for querying and analysis.

Real-World Example: E-Commerce Knowledge Graph

Let's say you're building a knowledge graph for an online store. Your data sources might include:

- A product catalog in a relational database.

- Customer reviews in JSON files.

- Supplier information in spreadsheets.

The ETL process for integrating this data might look like this:

1. Extract product data with SQL queries and customer reviews using Python's json module.

2. Transform the data to standardize categories and clean up review text.

3. Load the data into a graph database like Neo4j or an RDF store.

In Neo4j, you could use Cypher queries to load and link entities:

```
LOAD CSV WITH HEADERS FROM "file:///products.csv"
AS row
CREATE (p:Product {id: row.ProductID, name:
row.ProductName, category: row.Category, price:
row.Price});
```

Challenges and Best Practices

Data integration and preparation come with challenges, such as:

- Handling incomplete data: Use default values or infer missing information when possible.

- Resolving entity conflicts: When multiple sources reference the same entity, merge them based on unique identifiers like product IDs or patient IDs.

- Ensuring data quality: Regularly validate data to ensure consistency and accuracy.

Best practices include:

- Automating ETL processes with tools like Apache NiFi or Talend.

- Using logging and monitoring to track data integration pipelines.

- Documenting data mappings and transformations for transparency.

Data integration and preparation are essential steps in building a knowledge graph that accurately represents the real world. By extracting, transforming, and loading data from diverse sources, you create a unified graph that is clean, consistent, and ready for querying. These processes ensure that your knowledge graph is a reliable foundation for reasoning, analysis, and decision-making.

4.2 Knowledge Graph Platforms and Tools

Building and managing a knowledge graph requires a set of robust platforms and tools that simplify tasks like data storage, querying, visualization, and reasoning. The choice of platform significantly impacts your graph's scalability, performance, and ease of use. In this section, I'll guide you through the leading platforms and tools for creating knowledge graphs, explaining their features and demonstrating how to use them effectively.

A knowledge graph platform is a system or toolset designed to create, manage, and query graphs. These platforms provide features like:

- Graph storage: Efficiently storing large-scale graphs with millions or billions of nodes and edges.

- Querying capabilities: Allowing you to extract insights using graph-specific languages like SPARQL or Cypher.

- Reasoning support: Enabling the inference of new knowledge based on existing data and rules.

- Visualization tools: Providing ways to visually explore and analyze graphs.

The choice of platform depends on factors like your graph's size, complexity, and the standards you intend to follow (e.g., RDF, property graphs).

Types of Knowledge Graph Platforms

There are two primary types of knowledge graph platforms based on the underlying data model:

1. **RDF-based platforms:** These adhere to semantic web standards like RDF, OWL, and SPARQL.

2. **Property graph platforms:** These focus on nodes, edges, and their properties without enforcing semantic web standards.

Let's explore both in detail.

RDF-Based Platforms

RDF (Resource Description Framework) is a standard for representing data as triples (subject, predicate, object). Platforms that support RDF are ideal for knowledge graphs requiring semantic reasoning and interoperability.

GraphDB

GraphDB, developed by Ontotext, is a semantic graph database built for RDF data. It supports SPARQL for querying and OWL for reasoning.

Key Features:

- Scalable RDF storage.

- Built-in reasoning engine for semantic inference.

- SPARQL endpoint for querying.

Example Use Case: Suppose you have an ontology describing movies, directors, and actors. You can use GraphDB to store this data and query relationships like, "Which actors worked with Christopher Nolan?"

Setup Example:

```
PREFIX ex: <http://example.org/>

INSERT DATA {
  ex:Inception ex:directedBy ex:ChristopherNolan .
  ex:LeonardoDiCaprio ex:actedIn ex:Inception .
}
```

```
To query:
SELECT ?actor
WHERE {
  ?actor ex:actedIn ex:Inception .
}
```

Apache Jena

Apache Jena is an open-source framework for building semantic web applications. It includes a SPARQL query engine and tools for working with RDF and OWL.

Key Features:

- API for managing RDF data.

- SPARQL query engine (ARQ).

- Ontology support with OWL reasoning.

Example: Creating a Knowledge Graph with Jena

```
import org.apache.jena.rdf.model.*;
import org.apache.jena.vocabulary.RDF;

public class KnowledgeGraphExample {
    public static void main(String[] args) {
        Model model =
ModelFactory.createDefaultModel();

        // Define namespaces
        String namespace = "http://example.org/";
        Resource movie =
model.createResource(namespace + "Inception");
        Property directedBy =
model.createProperty(namespace + "directedBy");
        Resource director =
model.createResource(namespace +
"ChristopherNolan");

        // Add triple
        model.add(movie, directedBy, director);
```

```
// Print the graph
model.write(System.out, "TURTLE");
    }
}
```

Property Graph Platforms

Property graphs are node- and edge-centric, where both nodes and edges can have attributes. These platforms are intuitive and widely used for large-scale graphs.

Neo4j

Neo4j is one of the most popular graph databases, offering excellent visualization tools and the Cypher query language for working with property graphs.

Key Features:

- High performance for large graphs.

- Intuitive Cypher query language.

- Visualization tools for exploring data.

Example: Movie Knowledge Graph

```
CREATE (m:Movie {title: "Inception", releaseYear:
2010})
CREATE (d:Director {name: "Christopher Nolan"})
CREATE (a:Actor {name: "Leonardo DiCaprio"})
CREATE (a)-[:ACTED_IN]->(m)
CREATE (d)-[:DIRECTED]->(m)
```

To query all actors who acted in "Inception":

```
MATCH (a:Actor)-[:ACTED_IN]->(m:Movie {title:
"Inception"})
RETURN a.name
```

Output:

Leonardo DiCaprio

Amazon Neptune

Amazon Neptune is a fully managed graph database service that supports both RDF and property graphs. It's ideal for scalable, cloud-based applications.

Key Features:

- Support for SPARQL and Gremlin query languages.

- Managed service with high availability.

- Integration with AWS ecosystem.

Example: Using SPARQL in Amazon Neptune

```
PREFIX ex: <http://example.org/>

SELECT ?actor
WHERE {
  ?actor ex:actedIn ex:Inception .
}
```

Visualization Tools

Visualization tools help you explore the structure and relationships in your graph. They're especially useful for presentations and understanding complex graphs.

Neo4j Bloom

Neo4j Bloom provides an interactive, visual interface for querying and exploring graphs in Neo4j. You can write natural language queries or use Cypher to visualize results.

Gephi

Gephi is an open-source tool for graph visualization and analysis. You can import data from various formats, including CSV and Neo4j exports, to create dynamic visualizations.

Example: Visualizing a Graph

1. Export data from your knowledge graph to a CSV file.

2. Import the CSV into Gephi.

3. Use layout algorithms like ForceAtlas2 to create an interactive graph.

Choosing the Right Platform

When selecting a platform, consider these factors:

- Scalability: If your graph is expected to grow, choose a scalable platform like Amazon Neptune.

- Querying needs: Use RDF platforms like GraphDB for SPARQL queries or Neo4j for property graph queries.

- Ease of use: For beginners, Neo4j's intuitive interface is an excellent choice.

- Reasoning capabilities: If semantic reasoning is crucial, opt for GraphDB or Apache Jena.

Real-World Example: Social Network Analysis

Let's say you're building a knowledge graph for a social network. You can use Neo4j to model users, friendships, and interests:

- Nodes: User, Interest

- Edges: FRIENDS_WITH, INTERESTED_IN

Cypher query to find mutual friends:

```
MATCH (u1:User {name: "Alice"})-[:FRIENDS_WITH]-
(mutual)-[:FRIENDS_WITH]-(u2:User {name: "Bob"})
RETURN mutual.name
```

This query retrieves all mutual friends between Alice and Bob, helping you uncover connections in the network.

Knowledge graph platforms and tools form the backbone of any graph-based application. Whether you choose an RDF-based platform like GraphDB or a property graph database like Neo4j, understanding their features and capabilities is essential. With the right tools, you can efficiently store, query, and visualize your graph, unlocking the full potential of connected data for real-world applications.

4.3 Querying and Reasoning

Once your knowledge graph is built, the real value comes from interacting with it. Querying allows you to extract meaningful information, while reasoning helps uncover implicit knowledge that isn't explicitly stored in the graph. Together, these capabilities transform your knowledge graph from a static repository of data into a powerful tool for analysis, decision-making, and discovery.

Querying is the process of retrieving information from a knowledge graph. A query might ask for specific entities, relationships, or patterns, such as:

- "Who directed the movie Inception?"

- "What are the top-rated products in the Electronics category?"

The language used to query a knowledge graph depends on the platform and data model:

- RDF-based graphs use **SPARQL**.

- Property graphs use **Cypher** (Neo4j) or **Gremlin**.

SPARQL: Querying RDF Knowledge Graphs

SPARQL (SPARQL Protocol and RDF Query Language) is the standard language for querying RDF-based knowledge graphs. It works by matching patterns in the graph to the query's structure.

Example 1: Simple Query

Let's query a knowledge graph of movies to find all movies directed by Christopher Nolan.

Graph Data (in Turtle format):

```
@prefix ex: <http://example.org/> .

ex:Inception ex:directedBy ex:ChristopherNolan .
ex:Interstellar ex:directedBy ex:ChristopherNolan .
ex:ThePrestige ex:directedBy ex:ChristopherNolan .

SPARQL Query:
PREFIX ex: <http://example.org/>
```

```
SELECT ?movie
WHERE {
  ?movie ex:directedBy ex:ChristopherNolan .
}
```

Result:

movie

http://example.org/Inception

http://example.org/Interstellar

http://example.org/ThePrestige

This query looks for all triples where the predicate is ex:directedBy and the object is ex:ChristopherNolan, returning the matching subjects (movies).

Example 2: Filtering Results

Suppose each movie has a release year, and you want to find Christopher Nolan's movies released after 2010.

Graph Data:

```
ex:Inception ex:directedBy ex:ChristopherNolan ;
             ex:releaseYear "2010"^^xsd:integer .
ex:Interstellar ex:directedBy ex:ChristopherNolan ;
                ex:releaseYear "2014"^^xsd:integer

ex:ThePrestige ex:directedBy ex:ChristopherNolan ;
               ex:releaseYear "2006"^^xsd:integer .
```

SPARQL Query:

```
PREFIX ex: <http://example.org/>
PREFIX xsd: <http://www.w3.org/2001/XMLSchema#>

SELECT ?movie ?year
WHERE {
  ?movie ex:directedBy ex:ChristopherNolan ;
         ex:releaseYear ?year .
```

```
   FILTER (?year > 2010)
}

Result:
movie                                    year

http://example.org/Interstellar    2014
```

The FILTER clause restricts the results to movies released after 2010.

Cypher: Querying Property Graphs

Cypher is the query language used by Neo4j and is highly intuitive for working with property graphs. It uses pattern matching to traverse the graph.

Example 1: Simple Query

Let's query a property graph of movies and directors to find all movies directed by Christopher Nolan.

Graph Structure (Cypher commands to create the graph):

```
CREATE (m1:Movie {title: "Inception"})-
[:DIRECTED_BY]->(d:Director {name: "Christopher
Nolan"});
CREATE (m2:Movie {title: "Interstellar"})-
[:DIRECTED_BY]->(d);
CREATE (m3:Movie {title: "The Prestige"})-
[:DIRECTED_BY]->(d);
```

Query:

```
MATCH (m:Movie)-[:DIRECTED_BY]->(d:Director {name:
"Christopher Nolan"})
RETURN m.title
```

Result:

title

Inception

Interstellar

The Prestige

Example 2: Aggregating Data

Suppose each movie has a rating property, and you want to calculate the average rating of Christopher Nolan's movies.

Graph Update:

```
MATCH (m:Movie)
SET m.rating = CASE m.title
  WHEN "Inception" THEN 8.8
  WHEN "Interstellar" THEN 8.6
  WHEN "The Prestige" THEN 8.5
END;
```

Query:

```
MATCH (m:Movie)-[:DIRECTED_BY]->(d:Director {name:
"Christopher Nolan"})
RETURN AVG(m.rating) AS averageRating
```

Result:

averageRating

8.633333

Cypher's aggregation functions like AVG, SUM, and COUNT make it easy to analyze graph data.

Reasoning in Knowledge Graphs

Reasoning involves deriving new facts from existing data based on predefined rules. This is where the semantic power of RDF and OWL ontologies shines.

Example: Inferring Relationships

Let's define an ontology where:

1. All movies have a genre.

2. If a movie belongs to the genre "Sci-Fi," it can be inferred that the movie is a "Science Fiction Film."

Ontology in OWL (Turtle format):

```
@prefix ex: <http://example.org/> .
@prefix rdf: <http://www.w3.org/1999/02/22-rdf-
syntax-ns#> .
@prefix owl: <http://www.w3.org/2002/07/owl#> .

ex:SciFi rdf:type owl:Class .
ex:ScienceFictionFilm rdf:type owl:Class ;
                      owl:equivalentClass [
owl:intersectionOf (ex:SciFi) ] .
```

Graph Data:

```
ex:Inception rdf:type ex:SciFi .

A reasoning engine like Pellet or HermiT can infer:
ex:Inception rdf:type ex:ScienceFictionFilm .
```

This allows you to query for "Science Fiction Films" without explicitly tagging them in the graph.

Practical Exercise: Fraud Detection

In a banking knowledge graph, you might model accounts, transactions, and customers. Reasoning could help detect fraud by identifying unusual patterns.

Graph Data (Cypher):

```
CREATE (a1:Account {id: "A1", balance: 5000});
CREATE (a2:Account {id: "A2", balance: 100});
CREATE (a1)-[:TRANSFERRED {amount: 4900}]->(a2);
```

Query to Identify Suspicious Transfers:

```
MATCH (a1:Account)-[t:TRANSFERRED]->(a2:Account)
WHERE t.amount > 0.9 * a1.balance
```

```
RETURN a1.id, a2.id, t.amount
```

Result:

a1.id a2.id t.amount

A1   A2   4900

Reasoning can complement queries by detecting scenarios like frequent high-value transfers between the same accounts.

Querying and reasoning are the lifeblood of knowledge graphs, turning static data into actionable insights. SPARQL and Cypher allow you to explore relationships, analyze patterns, and answer complex questions with ease. Reasoning adds another layer by inferring new knowledge, enhancing the graph's intelligence and value. Together, these capabilities make knowledge graphs indispensable for solving real-world problems in domains like e-commerce, healthcare, and fraud detection.

Chapter 5: Applications and Advanced Topics

Knowledge graphs have found applications across industries, enabling smarter systems, deeper insights, and more intuitive user experiences. As their adoption grows, so does the need to address challenges related to scalability, optimization, and integration with artificial intelligence. In this chapter, we'll explore the practical applications of knowledge graphs, techniques to handle large-scale graphs, and their intersection with AI technologies.

5.1 Applications of Knowledge Graphs

Knowledge graphs are not just technical constructs; they are powerful tools that solve real-world problems by organizing and connecting information in meaningful ways. Their flexibility and capability to handle complex relationships make them invaluable across industries. In this section, I'll explore the applications of knowledge graphs, walking you through practical use cases with examples that show their transformative potential.

1. Search Engines and Enhanced Information Retrieval

Search engines have been one of the earliest and most impactful adopters of knowledge graphs. By connecting entities and relationships, search engines can provide precise answers rather than a list of links.

Example: Google Knowledge Graph
 When you search for "Leonardo da Vinci," Google doesn't just show links; it provides a knowledge panel with:

- His biography.

- His famous works like the *Mona Lisa* and *The Last Supper*.

- Related entities like "Renaissance artists" or "inventions."

This is possible because the knowledge graph understands that "Leonardo da Vinci" is an entity, and it connects his relationships to other entities like "art" and "science."

Practical Demonstration: Building a Mini Search System

Suppose you have a knowledge graph of books, authors, and genres. You want to implement a system that answers queries like, "Who wrote *1984*?"

Graph Data (RDF/Turtle):

```
@prefix ex: <http://example.org/> .

ex:1984 ex:writtenBy ex:GeorgeOrwell .
ex:GeorgeOrwell ex:bornIn ex:India .
ex:1984 ex:belongsToGenre ex:Dystopian .
```

SPARQL Query to Retrieve the Author:

```
PREFIX ex: <http://example.org/>

SELECT ?author
WHERE {
  ex:1984 ex:writtenBy ?author .
}
```

Result:

author

http://example.org/GeorgeOrwell

This approach makes search systems more intelligent by linking related entities and retrieving answers quickly.

2. Recommendation Systems

Knowledge graphs enable highly personalized recommendation systems by connecting users, products, and preferences.

Example: Netflix and Spotify

Netflix uses a knowledge graph to recommend movies and TV shows based on a user's viewing history and preferences. Similarly, Spotify connects users, songs, artists, and genres to suggest music tailored to each listener.

Building a Recommendation System

Let's consider a movie recommendation system. The knowledge graph links:

- Users to movies they've watched.
- Movies to genres.
- Genres to other related genres.

Cypher Query in Neo4j:

```
MATCH (user:User {id: "U1"})-[:WATCHED]->(m:Movie)-
[:BELONGS_TO]->(g:Genre)
MATCH (g)<-[:BELONGS_TO]-(rec:Movie)
WHERE NOT (user)-[:WATCHED]->(rec)
RETURN rec.title AS RecommendedMovies
```

This query retrieves movies in genres the user likes but hasn't watched yet.

3. Healthcare and Biomedical Research

In healthcare, knowledge graphs integrate patient data, medical research, and clinical guidelines to improve diagnostics, treatment, and research.

Example: Disease-Symptom Knowledge Graph

A graph connects:

- Diseases to their symptoms.
- Symptoms to treatments.
- Treatments to potential side effects.

Use Case: Diagnostic Assistance

If a patient presents with fever and cough, the graph can suggest possible diseases like influenza or COVID-19 based on their relationships to these symptoms.

SPARQL Query for Diagnosis:

```
PREFIX ex: <http://example.org/>

SELECT ?disease
```

```
WHERE {
    ?disease ex:hasSymptom ex:Fever .
    ?disease ex:hasSymptom ex:Cough .
}
```

This structured approach aids doctors by narrowing down potential diagnoses, speeding up the decision-making process.

4. Fraud Detection in Finance

Financial institutions use knowledge graphs to detect fraud by analyzing transactions, customer data, and account relationships.

Example: Transaction Graph

Nodes represent accounts, and edges represent transactions. By identifying patterns like frequent high-value transfers between accounts or connections to flagged accounts, banks can flag suspicious activity.

Neo4j Query for Fraud Detection:

```
MATCH (a1:Account)-[t:TRANSFERRED]->(a2:Account)
WHERE t.amount > 10000 AND a2.flagged = true
RETURN a1.id, a2.id, t.amount
```

This query detects large transfers to flagged accounts, helping to prevent fraud before it escalates.

5. E-Commerce: Product Search and Recommendations

E-commerce platforms use knowledge graphs to enhance product search and recommendations. By linking products, categories, and user preferences, they provide a personalized shopping experience.

Example: Amazon

Amazon's knowledge graph connects:

- Products to categories, reviews, and customer purchase histories.

- Customers to preferences and browsing behaviors.

Querying an E-Commerce Knowledge Graph

Let's query for related products in the same category as a smartphone.

Cypher Query:

```
MATCH (p:Product {name: "Smartphone"})-
[:BELONGS_TO]->(c:Category)<-[:BELONGS_TO]-
(related:Product)
RETURN related.name AS RelatedProducts
```

This query retrieves products in the same category as the smartphone, enhancing cross-selling opportunities.

6. Social Network Analysis

Social networks are inherently graphs, making them a natural fit for knowledge graphs. Platforms like Facebook and LinkedIn use knowledge graphs to model users, their relationships, and their interests.

Example: LinkedIn

LinkedIn's graph connects:

- Professionals to their skills, jobs, and connections.
- Companies to employees and job openings.

This enables features like:

- "People You May Know."
- Job recommendations based on skills and connections.

Querying a Social Network

Suppose you want to find mutual connections between two users.

Cypher Query:

```
MATCH (u1:User {name: "Alice"})-[:CONNECTED_TO]-
(mutual)-[:CONNECTED_TO]-(u2:User {name: "Bob"})
RETURN mutual.name AS MutualConnections
```

This query enhances networking opportunities by uncovering shared connections.

7. Knowledge Management and Enterprise Search

Organizations use knowledge graphs to unify and manage knowledge scattered across documents, databases, and systems. These graphs enable enterprise search, helping employees find relevant information quickly.

Example: Internal Knowledge Graph

An enterprise knowledge graph connects:

- Employees to projects, documents, and skills.

- Projects to clients and deliverables.

SPARQL Query for Employee Expertise:

```
PREFIX ex: <http://example.org/>

SELECT ?employee
WHERE {
  ?employee ex:hasSkill ex:DataScience .
  ?employee ex:workedOn ?project .
  ?project ex:deliveredTo ex:ClientA .
}
```

This query retrieves employees with data science expertise who have worked on projects for Client A.

8. Artificial Intelligence and Explainability

AI models often operate as black boxes, but knowledge graphs can make them more interpretable. By connecting input features to predictions, knowledge graphs explain why a model made a certain decision.

Example: Healthcare AI

An AI predicts a high risk of heart disease for a patient. The knowledge graph explains the prediction by linking:

- The patient's symptoms and medical history.

- Risk factors like age and cholesterol levels.

This transparency builds trust in AI systems, especially in critical domains like healthcare.

The applications of knowledge graphs span industries, from healthcare and finance to e-commerce and AI. They enhance search, enable personalized recommendations, improve diagnostics, and make AI models more interpretable. With their ability to represent complex relationships and uncover hidden insights, knowledge graphs are not just tools—they're catalysts for innovation in solving real-world problems. By mastering these applications, you can unlock the full potential of knowledge graphs in your own projects.

5.2 Scalability and Optimization

As knowledge graphs grow in size and complexity, handling them efficiently becomes a critical challenge. A graph with millions or billions of nodes and edges needs to be stored, queried, and maintained without compromising performance. Scalability and optimization ensure that your knowledge graph remains functional, fast, and reliable as it expands.

Scalability is the ability of a system to handle increased workloads without significant degradation in performance. For knowledge graphs, this means:

- Supporting large volumes of data (nodes, edges, and properties).

- Handling complex queries across vast relationships.

- Ensuring quick responses even as the graph grows.

Scalability isn't just about adding more resources—it's about optimizing the graph's design, storage, and query processes.

Challenges in Scaling Knowledge Graphs

1. Data Volume: Large graphs with billions of nodes and edges require efficient storage mechanisms. Without optimization, storage costs and retrieval times can skyrocket.

2. Query Complexity: As the graph grows, queries traversing multiple hops or relationships can become slower, especially if the graph isn't indexed effectively.

3. Distributed Systems: When a graph exceeds the capacity of a single server, it must be distributed across multiple nodes. Maintaining consistency and performance in distributed systems is challenging.

4. Dynamic Updates: Graphs often evolve, with new data being added and old data being updated or deleted. Managing these changes without disrupting queries is crucial.

Techniques for Scalability

1. Indexing for Faster Queries: Indexing accelerates query performance by organizing data for quick retrieval. Most graph databases support indexing on nodes and edges.

Example: Creating an Index in Neo4j

```
CREATE INDEX FOR (n:Person) ON (n.name)
```

This index ensures that queries filtering nodes by the name property are faster.

Query Without Index:

```
MATCH (p:Person {name: "Alice"}) RETURN p
```

If the graph has millions of nodes, searching without an index means scanning the entire graph, which is slow. With an index, the database locates the node in milliseconds.

2. Sharding for Distributed Storage: Sharding splits a large graph into smaller, manageable pieces stored across multiple servers. Each shard contains a subset of nodes and edges, often divided by logical partitions like geographic regions or entity types.

Example: Social Network Sharding

A global social network graph might be divided into shards by continent:

- Shard 1: Users in North America.

- Shard 2: Users in Europe.

This way, most queries (e.g., "Who are Alice's friends?") are contained within a single shard, reducing cross-shard communication.

Tools Supporting Sharding:

- **TigerGraph** provides built-in support for distributed graph processing.

- **Neo4j Fabric** allows querying across multiple graphs (shards).

3. Caching for Frequently Queried Data: Caching stores the results of frequent queries, reducing the need to repeatedly execute them on the database.

Example: E-Commerce Knowledge Graph

- A query like "Top 10 products in the Electronics category" might be run frequently.

- Instead of recalculating the results every time, cache them in memory and update periodically.

Using a caching layer like Redis alongside your graph database can drastically improve response times.

4. Parallel Processing for Query Execution: Parallel processing splits a query into smaller tasks that run simultaneously across multiple processors or servers.

Example: Using Apache Spark for Distributed Graph Processing

Apache Spark's GraphX library processes large graphs in parallel, making it ideal for tasks like PageRank or community detection.

Spark Code Example:

```
from pyspark import SparkContext
```

```
from pyspark.sql import SparkSession
from graphframes import GraphFrame

# Initialize Spark
sc = SparkContext.getOrCreate()
spark = SparkSession(sc)

# Create nodes and edges
nodes = spark.createDataFrame([
    ("1", "Alice"),
    ("2", "Bob"),
    ("3", "Charlie")
], ["id", "name"])

edges = spark.createDataFrame([
    ("1", "2", "follows"),
    ("2", "3", "follows"),
    ("3", "1", "follows")
], ["src", "dst", "relationship"])

# Create GraphFrame
graph = GraphFrame(nodes, edges)

# Run PageRank
pagerank = graph.pageRank(resetProbability=0.15,
maxIter=10)
pagerank.vertices.show()
```

5. Graph Partitioning

Partitioning divides a graph into smaller subgraphs to improve performance and scalability. Effective partitioning minimizes the number of edges crossing between partitions.

Example: Partitioning a Transportation Graph
In a graph representing a transportation network, partitioning by geographic region ensures that most queries (e.g., "Find routes in New York") are confined to a single partition.

Partitioning tools like METIS or algorithms built into Apache Giraph can help optimize this process.

Optimizing Queries

Optimization isn't just about the graph's structure—it's also about writing efficient queries.

1. Avoid Over fetching Data: Only request the data you need. For example, if you're querying for a person's name, don't fetch all their properties.

Inefficient Query:

```
MATCH (p:Person {name: "Alice"}) RETURN p
```

This retrieves the entire node, including unnecessary properties.

Optimized Query:

```
MATCH (p:Person {name: "Alice"}) RETURN p.name
```

2. Use Shorter Traversal Paths: Deep traversal queries can be slow. If possible, design your graph to reduce traversal depth.

Example: Reducing Depth in a Recommendation Graph
Instead of traversing multiple hops (User -> Movie -> Genre -> Movie), add direct edges (User -> Genre) to simplify queries.

3. Profile and Monitor Queries: Most graph databases provide tools to analyze query performance. For example, Neo4j's PROFILE command shows the execution plan for a query, helping you identify bottlenecks.

Using PROFILE:

```
PROFILE MATCH (p:Person)-[:FRIENDS_WITH]->(f:Person) RETURN f
```

The output reveals details like execution time and memory usage, guiding optimization efforts.

Real-World Example: Optimizing a Knowledge Graph for Healthcare

A healthcare knowledge graph integrates patient data, diseases, and treatments. As the graph grows, optimization becomes crucial.

Problem:
Querying for treatments based on patient symptoms is slow because the graph has millions of nodes.

Solution:

Indexing: Index nodes representing symptoms and diseases.

CREATE INDEX FOR (n:Symptom) ON (n.name)

1. **Caching:** Store frequent queries like "Common treatments for fever" in Redis.

2. **Sharding:** Partition the graph by hospital or region to localize queries.

3. **Parallel Processing:** Use Apache Spark to compute large-scale analytics, such as identifying common treatment patterns across regions.

Scalability and optimization are critical for maintaining the performance and usability of large knowledge graphs. Techniques like indexing, sharding, caching, and partitioning ensure that your graph can handle growing data volumes and complex queries. By writing efficient queries and leveraging distributed systems, you can build scalable knowledge graphs that deliver value in real-world applications. These strategies not only enhance performance but also future-proof your graph for continuous growth.

5.3 AI and Knowledge Graphs

The integration of artificial intelligence (AI) and knowledge graphs has unlocked powerful new capabilities for reasoning, learning, and understanding. Knowledge graphs provide structured, contextualized data that enhances AI's decision-making, while AI can enrich knowledge graphs through automated data extraction, inference, and analysis. Together, they create systems that are smarter, more explainable, and more effective in solving complex real-world problems.

AI models, especially machine learning systems, often work with unstructured or semi-structured data. However, these models face challenges when it comes to context, reasoning, and explainability. Knowledge graphs address these challenges by:

- Structuring data into meaningful entities and relationships.
- Providing semantic context that aids reasoning and inference.
- Offering a transparent and interpretable framework for explaining AI decisions.

Conversely, AI strengthens knowledge graphs by:

- Automating the extraction of entities and relationships from unstructured data.
- Enriching graphs with new insights and connections through machine learning models.
- Using advanced algorithms to uncover patterns and predict future trends.

Enhancing Machine Learning with Knowledge Graphs

Knowledge graphs provide additional features and context for machine learning models, improving their accuracy and interpretability.

Example: Recommender Systems with Graph-Based Features

Consider a movie recommendation system. Instead of only using user ratings as input features, you can enhance the model by incorporating knowledge graph relationships like:

- "User A likes Action movies."
- "Movie X belongs to the Action genre."
- "Movie X stars Actor Y, whom User A follows."

Practical Implementation

Let's create a graph of movies, genres, and user preferences using Neo4j:

```
CREATE (u:User {name: "Alice"})
CREATE (m1:Movie {title: "Inception"})-
[:BELONGS_TO]->(:Genre {name: "Sci-Fi"})
```

```
CREATE (m2:Movie {title: "Interstellar"})-
[:BELONGS_TO]->(:Genre {name: "Sci-Fi"})
CREATE (u)-[:LIKES]->(:Genre {name: "Sci-Fi"})

You can extract graph-based features for a machine
learning model:
MATCH (u:User)-[:LIKES]->(g:Genre)<-[:BELONGS_TO]-
(m:Movie)
RETURN u.name AS user, m.title AS recommendedMovie
```

These features can then be used in a recommendation model,
combining user preferences with graph-derived insights.

Using Graph Embeddings for Machine Learning

Graph embeddings convert nodes and edges into numerical vectors
that capture the structure and semantics of the graph. These
embeddings are particularly useful in machine learning models.

Example: Node2Vec for Social Network Analysis

Let's say you're analyzing a social network. By generating embeddings
for users (nodes), you can predict relationships like friendships or
recommendations.

Python Example Using Node2Vec:

```python
from node2vec import Node2Vec
import networkx as nx

# Create a graph
G = nx.Graph()
G.add_edges_from([(1, 2), (2, 3), (3, 4), (4, 5)])

# Generate embeddings
node2vec = Node2Vec(G, dimensions=64,
walk_length=10, num_walks=100, workers=4)
model = node2vec.fit(window=5, min_count=1,
batch_words=4)

# Get embedding for a node
embedding = model.wv['1']
print(embedding)
```

These embeddings can be used in downstream tasks like clustering, classification, or link prediction.

Automating Knowledge Graph Construction with AI

Creating and maintaining knowledge graphs manually is time-consuming. AI simplifies this process through techniques like natural language processing (NLP) and entity recognition.

Example: Extracting Knowledge from Text

Suppose you have a research article that states: "Albert Einstein developed the theory of relativity." AI models can identify:

- Entities: "Albert Einstein" (Person), "theory of relativity" (Concept).

- Relationship: "developed."

Python Example Using SpaCy for Entity Extraction:

```
import spacy

# Load NLP model
nlp = spacy.load("en_core_web_sm")

# Text input
text = "Albert Einstein developed the theory of
relativity."

# Process the text
doc = nlp(text)

# Extract entities
for ent in doc.ents:
    print(ent.text, ent.label_)
```

You can use these extracted entities and relationships to populate your knowledge graph.

Semantic Reasoning with AI and Ontologies

Reasoning engines use the rules defined in ontologies to infer new knowledge from existing data. When integrated with AI, this capability becomes even more powerful.

Example: Reasoning in Healthcare

In a healthcare knowledge graph, you might define:

- Rule: "If a patient has a fever and a cough, suggest possible flu diagnosis."

- Ontology: A flu is classified as a viral disease.

Reasoning engines like Pellet or HermiT can automatically infer that a patient with specific symptoms might have the flu, enabling early intervention.

Knowledge Graphs for Explainable AI

One of the biggest challenges in AI is the "black box" nature of machine learning models. Knowledge graphs make AI more interpretable by linking inputs to decisions through explicit relationships.

Example: Explaining AI Predictions

Suppose an AI predicts that a patient is at high risk for heart disease. A knowledge graph can explain the prediction by linking:

- Symptoms: High cholesterol, hypertension.

- Risk factors: Age, family history.

SPARQL Query for Explanation:

```
PREFIX ex: <http://example.org/>

SELECT ?factor
WHERE {
  ex:HeartDisease ex:hasRiskFactor ?factor .
}
```

This query retrieves all known risk factors for heart disease, making the AI's prediction transparent and trustworthy.

Advanced AI Techniques with Knowledge Graphs

Graph Neural Networks (GNNs)

GNNs operate directly on graph structures, learning representations for nodes, edges, or entire graphs. They are particularly useful in applications like:

- Drug discovery: Predicting interactions between molecules.

- Fraud detection: Identifying suspicious transaction patterns.

Python Example Using PyTorch Geometric:

```
from torch_geometric.data import Data
import torch

# Define graph structure
edge_index = torch.tensor([[0, 1], [1, 2]],
dtype=torch.long)   # Edges
x = torch.tensor([[1], [2], [3]],
dtype=torch.float)   # Node features

# Create PyTorch Geometric graph
data = Data(x=x, edge_index=edge_index)

print(data)
```

This example creates a simple graph with node features, ready for training a GNN.

Real-World Applications of AI and Knowledge Graphs

1. Healthcare: AI models integrated with knowledge graphs can predict patient outcomes, suggest treatments, and identify high-risk individuals.

2. Finance: Fraud detection systems use AI and graphs to identify abnormal transaction patterns and predict risks.

3. E-commerce: AI-powered recommendation systems use knowledge graphs to personalize product suggestions based on user preferences and behaviors.

4. Smart Assistants: Virtual assistants like Siri and Alexa use knowledge graphs to understand and respond to user queries, connecting entities like people, places, and events.

The combination of AI and knowledge graphs is transforming how we analyze, interpret, and act on data. Knowledge graphs bring structure and semantics to AI systems, enhancing their reasoning, explainability, and efficiency. Meanwhile, AI automates graph creation and enrichment, uncovering patterns and insights that were previously hidden. Together, they create a foundation for smarter, more transparent, and more effective systems that address real-world challenges with precision and clarity.

Chapter 6: Challenges and Future Directions

Knowledge graphs have become an essential tool in many industries, enabling the organization and analysis of complex, interconnected data. However, designing and managing knowledge graphs is not without its challenges. Additionally, as technology evolves, the future of knowledge graphs promises even more transformative potential. In this chapter, we'll explore the hurdles you may encounter when working with knowledge graphs and discuss the exciting possibilities that lie ahead.

6.1 Challenges in Knowledge Graph Design

Designing a knowledge graph is a nuanced and multifaceted process. While the idea of representing real-world entities and their relationships in a graph structure is straightforward in concept, its practical execution involves a range of challenges that require careful consideration and technical expertise. In this section, we'll explore the major challenges in knowledge graph design, backed by real-world examples and actionable solutions.

Data Integration Complexity

One of the first challenges in building a knowledge graph is integrating data from diverse sources. Each source may have different formats, structures, and levels of completeness, making it difficult to align them into a unified graph.

Example Challenge:
You're creating a knowledge graph for a university. Your data comes from:

- A relational database containing student records.
- Excel sheets with course details.
- Unstructured PDF documents detailing faculty research projects.

Each data source has its own schema, and some fields may overlap or conflict. For example, a student's name in one source may be stored as "John Doe," while in another it appears as "Doe, John."

Solution:
To handle this complexity, you need an **ETL (Extract, Transform, Load)** pipeline that:

1. Extracts data from all sources.

2. Cleans and transforms it to match the ontology of your graph.

3. Loads it into the graph database.

Practical Example in Python:
Here's how you might extract and transform student data from a CSV file before adding it to your graph:

```python
import csv
from rdflib import Graph, URIRef, Literal,
Namespace

# Define namespaces
EX = Namespace("http://example.org/")

# Create an RDF graph
g = Graph()

# Read data from a CSV file
with open("students.csv", "r") as file:
    reader = csv.DictReader(file)
    for row in reader:
        student = URIRef(EX[row["StudentID"]])
        g.add((student, EX.name,
Literal(row["Name"])))
        g.add((student, EX.enrolledIn,
Literal(row["Course"])))

# Serialize the graph
print(g.serialize(format="turtle").decode("utf-8"))
```

This approach ensures that data from structured sources like CSV files can be consistently added to the knowledge graph.

Ontology Design and Alignment

The ontology is the backbone of any knowledge graph. Designing it involves defining the entities, relationships, and properties that will structure your data. Poorly designed ontologies can lead to inconsistent graphs, difficulty in querying, and scalability issues.

Example Challenge:
You're building a knowledge graph for an e-commerce platform. Should "Smartphones" and "Laptops" be defined as subclasses of "Electronics," or should they be independent categories? If you later decide to merge these categories, it could disrupt existing queries and relationships.

Solution:
Start with a clear understanding of your domain and its requirements. Use existing ontologies as a baseline (e.g., Schema.org for e-commerce) and extend them as needed.

Using OWL to Define Ontologies:

```
@prefix ex: <http://example.org/> .
@prefix owl: <http://www.w3.org/2002/07/owl#> .

ex:Electronics rdf:type owl:Class .
ex:Smartphone rdf:type owl:Class ;
               rdfs:subClassOf ex:Electronics .
ex:Laptop rdf:type owl:Class ;
          rdfs:subClassOf ex:Electronics .
```

This structure ensures that changes can be accommodated with minimal disruption.

Ensuring Data Consistency

Inconsistent data can lead to erroneous inferences and unreliable insights. Common consistency issues include:

- Duplicate nodes representing the same entity.

- Conflicting relationships or properties.

- Missing or incomplete data.

Example Challenge:
A knowledge graph for a hospital has duplicate nodes for the same doctor:

- Dr. John Smith

- Dr. J. Smith

If these nodes aren't resolved, queries about this doctor may yield incomplete results.

Solution:
Use entity resolution techniques to identify and merge duplicates. Tools like Dedupe or custom algorithms based on similarity scores (e.g., Levenshtein distance) can help.

Python Example for Entity Resolution:

```python
from fuzzywuzzy import fuzz

# Define entities
entities = ["Dr. John Smith", "Dr. J. Smith", "Dr. Jane Doe"]

# Check for duplicates
for i, e1 in enumerate(entities):
    for e2 in entities[i + 1:]:
        similarity = fuzz.ratio(e1, e2)
        if similarity > 80:
            print(f"Possible duplicate: {e1} and {e2} (Similarity: {similarity}%)")
```

Query Performance Optimization

As the graph grows, complex queries can become slow, especially those involving deep traversals or large subgraphs. For instance, a query that retrieves all authors who co-authored papers on AI with another author might traverse hundreds of nodes.

Example Challenge:
In a research knowledge graph, a query to find all co-authors of "Dr. Alice" who also collaborated with "Dr. Bob" takes several seconds to execute on a large graph.

Solution:

- Index frequently queried properties to speed up lookups.

- Optimize queries by narrowing the scope where possible.

- Use caching for repetitive queries.

Indexing Example in Neo4j:

CREATE INDEX FOR (n:Author) ON (n.name)

Scalability and Distributed Systems

Scaling a knowledge graph to billions of nodes and edges often requires distributed systems. However, distributing the graph introduces challenges like ensuring data locality and minimizing cross-shard queries.

Example Challenge:
A global social network graph with billions of users must handle queries like "Find all friends of friends of Alice." If Alice's friends are spread across multiple shards, the query performance can degrade.

Solution:
Partition the graph logically to minimize cross-shard communication. For example, partition a social network graph by geographic regions or user communities.

Real-World Tool:
Amazon Neptune and TigerGraph support distributed graph storage and query processing, making them ideal for large-scale applications.

Managing Dynamic Graphs

Knowledge graphs are rarely static. New entities and relationships are added, and outdated data must be removed. Keeping the graph up to date without introducing inconsistencies is a significant challenge.

Example Challenge:
In a knowledge graph for news articles, new events are constantly added while older articles become less relevant.

Solution:
- Implement event-driven updates to reflect real-time changes.

- Define expiration rules for stale data.

Example of Event-Driven Update in Neo4j:

```
MATCH (n:Article)
WHERE n.timestamp < timestamp() - 30 * 24 * 60 * 60
* 1000   // Older than 30 days
DETACH DELETE n
```

Interoperability and Standards

Many organizations use proprietary schemas or tools, making it hard to integrate multiple knowledge graphs. For example, a healthcare graph using SNOMED CT might not be easily compatible with an e-commerce graph based on Schema.org.

Solution:
Adopt and adhere to widely accepted standards like RDF, OWL, and SPARQL. Use ontology alignment tools to map schemas across domains.

Designing a knowledge graph is an intricate process that demands attention to detail at every step. From integrating diverse data sources to optimizing query performance and managing scalability, each challenge requires thoughtful solutions. By understanding these challenges and leveraging the right tools and techniques, you can build knowledge graphs that are not only functional but also scalable, consistent, and impactful. As you address these hurdles, your graph will become a powerful asset capable of solving complex, real-world problems with clarity and precision.

6.2 Future of Knowledge Graphs

Knowledge graphs are becoming essential tools in technology and data-driven industries. They represent and link information in a structured way, enabling better understanding, reasoning, and insights. As technology evolves, knowledge graphs are set to play an even more significant role in solving complex problems and enhancing applications across various domains. In this section, we'll explore the emerging trends, advancements, and potential future directions of knowledge graphs.

A knowledge graph is a way of representing information as a network of entities (nodes) and their relationships (edges). Entities can be people, places, products, or abstract concepts, while relationships define how these entities are connected. For example, in a knowledge graph about movies:

- A node might represent a movie, director, or actor.

- An edge might represent the relationship "directed by" or "acted in."

Knowledge graphs make it easier to query and reason about data by organizing it into meaningful connections.

1. Enhanced Integration with Artificial Intelligence

One of the most significant trends in the future of knowledge graphs is their integration with artificial intelligence (AI). Knowledge graphs enhance AI models by providing structured, contextualized data that improves learning, reasoning, and explainability.

Explainable AI (XAI)

AI systems often function as black boxes, making it hard to understand how decisions are made. Knowledge graphs provide a framework for explaining AI decisions by linking inputs, processes, and outcomes in a clear, interpretable way.

Example:
 In healthcare, an AI system predicting a high risk of diabetes can use a knowledge graph to explain its reasoning:

- Input: The patient has high blood sugar and a sedentary lifestyle.

- Knowledge Graph: Links these factors to diabetes risk based on clinical studies.

Graph Neural Networks (GNNs)

Graph Neural Networks are a type of AI model designed to operate directly on graph structures. They learn patterns and representations from graphs, enabling applications like fraud detection, drug discovery, and social network analysis.

Future Direction:
 As GNNs become more sophisticated, they will enable advanced

analytics on large-scale knowledge graphs, uncovering patterns and relationships that were previously inaccessible.

2. Real-Time and Dynamic Knowledge Graphs

Traditional knowledge graphs are often static, meaning they are updated periodically rather than continuously. However, real-time applications such as fraud detection, personalized recommendations, and supply chain monitoring require dynamic knowledge graphs that can update and adapt instantly.

Streaming Data Integration

Dynamic knowledge graphs will incorporate data streams from IoT devices, APIs, and user interactions. For example, a logistics company could use a real-time knowledge graph to track shipments, monitor delays, and optimize routes.

Future Tools:
Platforms like **Apache Kafka** and **Amazon Kinesis** are already being integrated with graph databases to support real-time updates.

3. Enhanced Scalability

As knowledge graphs grow to billions or even trillions of nodes and edges, scalability becomes a critical challenge. The future of knowledge graphs will rely on advances in distributed computing, parallel processing, and optimized storage systems.

Cloud-Native Graph Databases

Graph databases are increasingly moving to the cloud to leverage distributed resources. Cloud-native systems like Amazon Neptune and Google BigQuery Graph allow developers to scale their knowledge graphs on demand without worrying about infrastructure constraints.

Partitioning and Sharding

Partitioning divides a large graph into smaller, manageable subgraphs, while sharding distributes these subgraphs across multiple servers. These techniques will continue to evolve, enabling efficient processing of massive graphs.

Example:
 A global social network graph might partition users by geographic region, ensuring that queries about friendships or recommendations are localized and fast.

4. Federated Knowledge Graphs

In the future, knowledge graphs will increasingly operate in federated ecosystems, where multiple organizations maintain their own graphs but connect them seamlessly for shared insights. This approach preserves data ownership while enabling collaboration.

Example: Healthcare and Research

Imagine hospitals, pharmaceutical companies, and research institutions maintaining their own knowledge graphs:

- A hospital graph contains patient data and treatment histories.

- A pharmaceutical graph links drugs to clinical trial results.

- A research graph links studies and publications.

A federated system could enable cross-querying these graphs to identify new treatment opportunities while maintaining data privacy.

Standardized Protocols

Federated graphs will rely on standardized protocols like SPARQL endpoints and ontology alignment tools to ensure interoperability.

5. Knowledge Graphs in Edge Computing

Edge computing brings computation closer to the data source, such as IoT devices or local servers, reducing latency and bandwidth usage. Knowledge graphs in edge environments will enable localized processing and real-time decision-making.

Example: Smart Cities

In a smart city, sensors on traffic lights, vehicles, and roads generate vast amounts of data. A localized knowledge graph at the edge could:

- Monitor traffic flow.

- Predict congestion.

- Suggest optimal routes to drivers.

By operating at the edge, these systems can provide instant insights without relying on a centralized server.

6. Semantic Search and Conversational AI

Knowledge graphs will continue to revolutionize search engines and conversational AI by enabling more intelligent and context-aware interactions.

Semantic Search

Semantic search uses a knowledge graph to understand the meaning behind a query, rather than matching keywords. For example:

- Query: "Who is the CEO of Tesla?"

- Knowledge Graph: Links Tesla to Elon Musk through the relationship "CEO."

This approach returns precise, contextually relevant answers.

Conversational AI

Virtual assistants like Siri and Alexa rely on knowledge graphs to answer questions and execute tasks. As knowledge graphs grow, these systems will become more capable of handling complex, multi-turn conversations.

7. Domain-Specific Knowledge Graphs

General-purpose knowledge graphs, like Google's Knowledge Graph, are incredibly useful but lack the depth required for specialized fields. The future will see a proliferation of domain-specific graphs tailored to industries such as:

- Healthcare: Linking diseases, symptoms, treatments, and research.

- Finance: Connecting stocks, companies, markets, and regulations.

- Education: Organizing courses, curriculums, and student progress.

These specialized graphs will enable more precise queries and insights within their respective domains.

8. Quantum Computing for Knowledge Graphs

Quantum computing holds the potential to transform how we process and analyze knowledge graphs. Quantum algorithms could solve graph-related problems, such as pathfinding and clustering, exponentially faster than classical methods.

Example: Drug Discovery

In drug discovery, a knowledge graph might link molecules, proteins, and diseases. Quantum computing could analyze these connections to identify potential treatments much faster than traditional methods.

The future of knowledge graphs is full of promise. They are set to become more dynamic, scalable, and integrated with advanced technologies like AI, edge computing, and quantum computing. By evolving to handle real-time data, operate in federated ecosystems, and support domain-specific applications, knowledge graphs will continue to transform how we organize and analyze complex information. Whether you're a developer, researcher, or decision-maker, the advancements in knowledge graphs will open new possibilities for smarter, more connected systems.

Chapter 7: Hands-On Guide

This chapter provides a practical, step-by-step guide to building a knowledge graph from scratch and offers best practices to ensure your project is efficient, scalable, and effective. Whether you're a beginner or experienced, the goal is to equip you with actionable techniques that bridge the gap between theory and implementation.

7.1 Step-by-Step Project Implementation

Building a knowledge graph from scratch can feel overwhelming, but breaking it into structured steps simplifies the process. Here, I'll guide you through implementing a knowledge graph project in a clear, detailed manner. Let's create a knowledge graph for a **university system** that connects students, courses, professors, and research projects. By the end of this walkthrough, you'll have a functional knowledge graph and a deep understanding of the process.

Step 1: Define the Purpose and Scope

Before you begin, clearly define what your knowledge graph will achieve and the scope of its data. This ensures your efforts remain focused and aligned with the project's goals.

Use Case Example:
 We want to create a knowledge graph that:

1. Helps students find courses, professors, and research projects matching their interests.

2. Provides administrators with insights into enrollment and teaching trends.

Step 2: Design the Ontology

An ontology defines the structure of your knowledge graph by specifying the types of entities, their relationships, and attributes.

Entities:

- **Student**: Attributes: id, name, major.

- **Professor**: Attributes: id, name, department.

- **Course**: Attributes: id, title, credits.

- **ResearchProject**: Attributes: id, title, focusArea.

Relationships:

- Student -> ENROLLED_IN -> Course
- Professor -> TEACHES -> Course
- Professor -> LEADS -> ResearchProject

Example Ontology in RDF (Turtle format):

@prefix ex: <http://example.org/> .

@prefix owl: <http://www.w3.org/2002/07/owl#> .

ex:Student rdf:type owl:Class .

ex:Professor rdf:type owl:Class .

ex:Course rdf:type owl:Class .

ex:ResearchProject rdf:type owl:Class .

ex:enrolledIn rdf:type owl:ObjectProperty ;

    rdfs:domain ex:Student ;

    rdfs:range ex:Course .

ex:teaches rdf:type owl:ObjectProperty ;

    rdfs:domain ex:Professor ;

    rdfs:range ex:Course .

ex:leads rdf:type owl:ObjectProperty ;

    rdfs:domain ex:Professor ;

    rdfs:range ex:ResearchProject .

This ontology serves as the backbone for your knowledge graph, guiding the organization of data and relationships.

Step 3: Collect and Prepare Data

Gather data from various sources. For our university system, the data might include:

- A CSV file with student details.

- A database with professor and course information.

- JSON files describing research projects.

Example: Sample Data (students.csv):

```
StudentID,Name,Major,CourseID
S1,Alice,Computer Science,C1
S2,Bob,Mathematics,C2
S3,Charlie,Physics,C1
```

Loading Data in Python: Here's how to load this data into an RDF graph using rdflib:

```python
import csv
from rdflib import Graph, URIRef, Literal, Namespace

# Define namespaces
EX = Namespace("http://example.org/")

# Create a graph
g = Graph()

# Load student data from CSV
with open("students.csv", "r") as file:
    reader = csv.DictReader(file)
    for row in reader:
        student = URIRef(EX[row["StudentID"]])
        course = URIRef(EX[row["CourseID"]])
        g.add((student, EX.name,
Literal(row["Name"])))
        g.add((student, EX.major,
Literal(row["Major"])))
```

```
        g.add((student, EX.enrolledIn, course))

# Serialize the graph
print(g.serialize(format="turtle").decode("utf-8"))
```

This script creates triples for each student and their enrollment in courses.

Step 4: Build the Knowledge Graph

Choose a graph database that suits your requirements. For this project, we'll use **Neo4j**, which is intuitive and offers powerful visualization tools.

Setting Up Neo4j:

1. Download and install Neo4j.

2. Open the Neo4j Desktop application and create a new project.

3. Start a database and open the Neo4j Browser.

Import Data into Neo4j: You can load the same data using Cypher, Neo4j's query language:

```
CREATE (:Student {id: "S1", name: "Alice", major:
"Computer Science"})-[:ENROLLED_IN]->(:Course {id:
"C1", title: "Data Science"})
CREATE (:Student {id: "S2", name: "Bob", major:
"Mathematics"})-[:ENROLLED_IN]->(:Course {id: "C2",
title: "Calculus"})
CREATE (:Professor {id: "P1", name: "Dr. Smith",
department: "Computer Science"})-[:TEACHES]-
>(:Course {id: "C1", title: "Data Science"})
CREATE (:Professor {id: "P2", name: "Dr. Johnson",
department: "Mathematics"})-[:LEADS]-
>(:ResearchProject {id: "R1", title: "AI for
Climate Change"})
```

Step 5: Query the Knowledge Graph

Once your graph is populated, querying it enables you to extract meaningful insights.

Find all courses a student is enrolled in:

```
MATCH (s:Student {name: "Alice"})-[:ENROLLED_IN]-
>(c:Course)
RETURN c.title
```

Find professors teaching courses in Computer Science:

```
MATCH (p:Professor)-[:TEACHES]->(c:Course)
WHERE p.department = "Computer Science"
RETURN p.name, c.title
```

Step 6: Visualize the Knowledge Graph

Visualization helps you explore and verify the structure of your graph. Neo4j's browser provides an interactive visualization of nodes and relationships. Run queries like:

```
MATCH (n) RETURN n
```

This query retrieves all nodes and relationships, allowing you to explore the graph visually.

Step 7: Refine and Scale

As your graph grows, consider the following:

Indexing: Speed up queries by indexing frequently searched properties.

```
CREATE INDEX FOR (n:Student) ON (n.name)
```

- **Dynamic Updates:** Automate the addition of new data through APIs or scheduled scripts.

- **Partitioning:** Split the graph into subgraphs if it becomes too large for a single instance.

Practical Exercise

Let's implement a query to find research projects related to a professor's courses:

```
MATCH (p:Professor {name: "Dr. Smith"})-[:TEACHES]-
>(c:Course)<-[:ENROLLED_IN]-(s:Student)
MATCH (p)-[:LEADS]->(r:ResearchProject)
```

```
RETURN s.name AS Student, c.title AS Course,
r.title AS ResearchProject
```

This query identifies students in Dr. Smith's courses and links them to his research projects.

Building a knowledge graph is a step-by-step process that starts with defining your goals and designing an ontology, followed by data integration, graph construction, and querying. By following this implementation guide, you can create a functional, meaningful knowledge graph that provides insights and solves real-world problems. With tools like Neo4j and Python libraries, the process becomes approachable and efficient, whether you're a beginner or an experienced developer.

7.2 Best Practices and Tips

Building and maintaining a knowledge graph is a complex task, and success often depends on following proven practices that ensure scalability, consistency, and effectiveness. In this section, I'll share comprehensive best practices and tips that can guide you through designing, implementing, and optimizing your knowledge graph. These insights are drawn from real-world applications and common challenges, making them relevant for both beginners and experienced practitioners.

1. Start with a Clear Use Case

Before building a knowledge graph, you need a well-defined purpose. Ask yourself:

- What problem does the knowledge graph solve?

- Who will use it, and what kind of queries will they run?

- What outcomes do you expect from the graph?

Example:
 If you're building a graph for an e-commerce platform, your use case might be:
 "Enable personalized product recommendations by connecting customers, products, categories, and reviews."

This clarity helps in designing an ontology that directly addresses your goals.

2. Design a Thoughtful Ontology

Your ontology is the foundation of the knowledge graph. It should reflect the real-world entities, relationships, and attributes relevant to your use case. A poorly designed ontology leads to inconsistent data and inefficient queries.

Tips for Ontology Design:

- Start simple: Focus on the most critical entities and relationships. For example, in an e-commerce graph, start with Customer, Product, and Category.

- Use existing standards: Adopt ontologies like Schema.org (general-purpose) or SNOMED CT (healthcare) when possible. These provide well-established structures that save time and ensure compatibility.

Example Ontology in Turtle Format:

```
@prefix ex: <http://example.org/> .
@prefix owl: <http://www.w3.org/2002/07/owl#> .

ex:Customer rdf:type owl:Class .
ex:Product rdf:type owl:Class .
ex:Category rdf:type owl:Class .

ex:buys rdf:type owl:ObjectProperty ;
        rdfs:domain ex:Customer ;
        rdfs:range ex:Product .

ex:belongsToCategory rdf:type owl:ObjectProperty ;
                     rdfs:domain ex:Product ;
                     rdfs:range ex:Category .
```

3. Normalize and Clean Data

Clean and consistent data is essential for building a reliable knowledge graph. Without proper cleaning, you risk introducing duplicate nodes, conflicting relationships, and inaccurate results.

Steps for Data Cleaning:

1. Remove duplicates: Merge duplicate entities, ensuring a single representation for each entity.

2. Standardize formats: Use consistent formats for dates, names, and other attributes. For instance, ensure all dates are stored as YYYY-MM-DD.

3. Handle missing values: Use defaults, infer values when possible, or flag incomplete data for further action.

Python Example for Data Cleaning:

```python
import pandas as pd

# Load data
data = pd.DataFrame({
    'ProductID': ['P1', 'P2', 'P2'],
    'ProductName': ['Laptop', 'Smartphone',
'Smartphone'],
    'Category': ['Electronics', 'Electronics',
None]
})

# Remove duplicates
data = data.drop_duplicates()

# Fill missing values
data['Category'] =
data['Category'].fillna('Unknown')

print(data)

This ensures clean, non-redundant data for your
graph.
```

4. Use Indexing for Faster Queries

As your graph grows, query performance becomes critical. Indexing frequently queried properties can significantly speed up lookups.

Example in Neo4j:

```
CREATE INDEX FOR (n:Product) ON (n.name)
```

If you frequently query products by name, this index reduces query execution time.

Before Indexing:

```
MATCH (p:Product {name: "Laptop"}) RETURN p
```

Without an index, Neo4j scans all nodes labeled Product, which is slow for large graphs.

5. Optimize Your Queries

Writing efficient queries can prevent performance bottlenecks. Here's how:

- Be specific: Only query the data you need. Avoid fetching unnecessary properties or relationships.

- Use constraints: Narrow down results with conditions like WHERE to reduce the graph traversal depth.

Example Query Optimization: Instead of:

```
MATCH (p:Product)-[:BELONGS_TO_CATEGORY]-
>(:Category {name: "Electronics"})
RETURN p

Add constraints:
MATCH (p:Product {name: "Laptop"})-
[:BELONGS_TO_CATEGORY]->(:Category {name:
"Electronics"})
RETURN p
```

This avoids traversing unrelated products, improving performance.

6. Regularly Validate and Update the Graph

Knowledge graphs are dynamic and require maintenance to remain accurate and useful. Periodically validate the graph to:

- Identify and remove outdated data.

- Ensure relationships are consistent with the ontology.

- Merge redundant or duplicate nodes.

Example: Removing Outdated Data in Neo4j:

```
MATCH (n:Product)
WHERE n.lastUpdated < date("2023-01-01")
DETACH DELETE n
```

This removes products that haven't been updated since a specific date.

7. Use Visualization for Exploration

Visualizing your graph helps in understanding its structure and spotting inconsistencies. Tools like **Neo4j Bloom** and **Gephi** make it easy to explore your data visually.

Example: Exploring Relationships in Neo4j Browser: Run:

MATCH (n)-[r]->(m)

RETURN n, r, m

This displays all nodes and relationships, helping you see how entities are connected.

8. Leverage Graph Embeddings for Advanced Analytics

Graph embeddings transform graph data into numerical vectors, enabling machine learning applications like clustering and classification. Libraries like **Node2Vec** and **PyTorch Geometric** simplify this process.

Example: Node2Vec for Social Networks:

```
from node2vec import Node2Vec
import networkx as nx

# Create a graph
G = nx.Graph()
G.add_edges_from([(1, 2), (2, 3), (3, 4)])

# Generate embeddings
node2vec = Node2Vec(G, dimensions=64,
walk_length=10, num_walks=100)
```

```
model = node2vec.fit(window=5)

# Get embedding for node 1
embedding = model.wv['1']
print(embedding)
```

This embedding can be used in downstream machine learning tasks.

9. Use Caching for Repeated Queries

Frequently run queries can benefit from caching. A caching layer reduces the load on your graph database and speeds up responses.

Example with Redis for Query Caching:

```
import redis

# Connect to Redis
cache = redis.Redis(host='localhost', port=6379)

# Store query result
cache.set("top_products", "[Laptop, Smartphone]")

# Retrieve cached result
print(cache.get("top_products"))
```

This approach ensures quick responses for repeated queries like "Top 10 products."

10. Document Your Graph

Documenting your knowledge graph ensures that your team understands its structure and usage. Include:

- A clear schema with entities, relationships, and attributes.

- Sample queries for common use cases.

- Data sources and their mapping to the ontology.

Example Schema Documentation:

Entity Type	Attributes	Relationships

Student	id, name, major	ENROLLED_IN (Course)
Course	id, title, credits	TAUGHT_BY (Professor)
Professor	id, name, department	LEADS (ResearchProject)

Creating and managing a knowledge graph is as much about process and discipline as it is about technology. By following these best practices—defining clear goals, designing an effective ontology, optimizing data and queries, and leveraging the right tools—you can ensure your graph is scalable, consistent, and valuable. These tips not only improve performance but also future-proof your knowledge graph, making it a powerful tool for solving complex, data-driven challenges.

Conclusion

Knowledge graphs have emerged as one of the most transformative tools in the era of interconnected and data-driven systems. By enabling the representation of complex relationships between entities, knowledge graphs bridge the gap between raw data and actionable insights, fostering innovation across industries such as healthcare, finance, e-commerce, and artificial intelligence.

This book has guided you through every aspect of knowledge graphs, from understanding their fundamental principles to implementing, scaling, and leveraging them for real-world applications. Whether you are a beginner curious about their potential or an experienced developer looking to refine your skills, the concepts, examples, and techniques presented here aim to equip you with the knowledge and confidence to build effective and impactful knowledge graphs.

What We've Learned

1. Foundational Concepts: We began with the basics—what knowledge graphs are, their history, and why they are crucial in modern systems. Understanding their structure as nodes, edges, and properties provided a strong starting point.

2. Core Components: From graph models to standards like RDF, OWL, and SPARQL, we explored the essential building blocks that make knowledge graphs robust, flexible, and interoperable.

3. Design and Implementation: Through a detailed step-by-step guide, you learned how to design an ontology, integrate data, and implement a knowledge graph using tools like Neo4j and Python libraries.

4. Applications and Advanced Topics: Real-world examples illustrated how knowledge graphs are transforming search engines, recommendation systems, fraud detection, and explainable AI. We also delved into scalability, optimization, and the synergies between AI and knowledge graphs.

5. Best Practices: Practical tips ensured that you could address common challenges such as data integration, query performance, and graph maintenance while adhering to industry standards and leveraging advanced tools.

The power of knowledge graphs lies in their ability to make sense of complexity. By structuring data into meaningful connections, they unlock new opportunities for understanding, reasoning, and innovation. They are not just tools but platforms for collaboration, enabling businesses, researchers, and developers to extract value from vast and diverse datasets.

As we move into a future dominated by artificial intelligence, real-time systems, and decentralized ecosystems, knowledge graphs will play an even greater role. Their integration with advanced technologies like graph neural networks, federated learning, and quantum computing will open doors to applications we are only beginning to imagine.

Your Journey Ahead

This book is not an endpoint but a foundation for your journey into the world of knowledge graphs. With the concepts and techniques you've learned, you can now:

- Build knowledge graphs tailored to specific domains and challenges.

- Leverage graph-based insights to solve complex problems.

- Stay at the forefront of this evolving field by adopting emerging tools and practices.

The world of knowledge graphs is vast and ever-growing, and your expertise can contribute to shaping its future. Whether you are building solutions that empower businesses, enhance user experiences, or advance scientific research, your knowledge graph projects have the potential to make a meaningful impact.

Knowledge graphs are more than a technical innovation—they are a mindset shift in how we think about data, relationships, and meaning. They encourage us to see the connections between things, to reason about the whole rather than the parts, and to derive insights that were previously hidden.

As you take what you've learned and apply it to your work, remember that the value of a knowledge graph lies not just in its data but in the questions, it can answer and the decisions it can guide. With curiosity, creativity, and a commitment to best practices, you can build systems that truly make data smarter.

Thank you for embarking on this exploration of knowledge graphs. The skills and insights you've gained here will not only advance your projects but also contribute to the broader evolution of connected, intelligent systems. The future is connected, and knowledge graphs are at the center of it all.

www.ingramcontent.com/pod-product-compliance
Lightning Source LLC
LaVergne TN
LVHW081530050326
832903LV00025B/1722